CULTURES OF THE WORLD
Zimbabwe

Cavendish
Square

New York

Published in 2014 by Cavendish Square Publishing, LLC
303 Park Avenue South, Suite 1247, New York, NY 10010

Third Edition

This publication is published with arrangement with Marshall Cavendish International (Asia) Pte Ltd.

Copyright © 2014 Marshall Cavendish International (Asia) Pte Ltd.

Website: cavendishsq.com

Cultures of the World is a registered trademark of Times Publishing Limited.

This publication represents the opinions and views of the author based on his or her personal experience, knowledge, and research. The information in this book serves as a general guide only. The author and publisher have used their best efforts in preparing this book and disclaim liability rising directly or indirectly from the use and application of this book.

CPSIA Compliance Information: Batch #WW14CSQ

All websites were available and accurate when this book was sent to press.

Library of Congress Cataloging-in-Publication Data
Sheehan, Sean.
Zimbabwe / by Sean Sheehan and Michael Spilling.
   p. cm. — (Cultures of the world)
Includes index.
ISBN 978-0-76148-017-4 (hardcover) ISBN 978-1-62712-628-1 (paperback) ISBN 978-0-76148-025-9 (ebook)
1. Zimbabwe — Juvenile literature. I. Sheehan, Sean, 1951- II. Title.
DT2889.S54 2014
968.91—d23

Writers: Sean Sheehan and Michael Spilling
Editor: Mindy Pang
Designer: Benson Tan

PICTURE CREDITS
Cover: © Chad Ehlers / Alamy
Audrius Tomonis – www.banknotes.com: 135 • Corbis / Click Photos: 64, 89 • Getty Images: 27, 35, 40, 83 •
Inmagine.com / Alamy: 1, 3, 5, 7, 8, 10, 12, 13, 14, 17, 18, 19, 20, 22, 24, 28, 29, 31, 34, 38, 42, 45, 48, 49, 50, 52, 54, 55, 57, 58, 59, 60, 61, 62, 63, 66, 67, 68, 70, 72, 73, 74, 75, 76, 77, 79, 80, 82, 84, 85, 87, 90, 91, 92, 94, 96, 97, 100, 101, 102, 104, 105, 106, 107, 110, 111, 112, 113, 114, 115, 116, 117, 122, 123, 124, 125, 126, 127, 128, 130, 131 • Reuters: 36, 119, 120

PRECEDING PAGE
An aerial view of the Inyanga Mutare Eastern Highlands of Zimbabwe.

Printed in the United States of America

CONTENTS

ZIMBABWE TODAY

FORMERLY KNOWN AS RHODESIA, THE STATE OF ZIMBABWE evokes wonder. Gold hunters have looked for the Biblical King Solomon's mines in Zimbabwe. Historians and archaeologists explore the nation's ancient sites to uncover clues about early humans. Nature lovers admire Zimbabwe's awesome wildlife, including one of the largest wild elephant populations in the world.

Political, economic, and social problems have put modern Zimbabwe in news headlines around the world. Zimbabwe's struggle to gain independence from Britain, establish a democratic government, and redistribute land have been accompanied by conflicts among the country's factions and ethnic groups.

Despite these problems, Zimbabwe remains one of the leading states of Africa. In their attempts to find a way to live and work together as fellow citizens, Zimbabweans have developed a unique culture and way of life.

After independence from the British in 1980, Zimbabwe was a new nation full of promise. Many believed it had a bright future ahead as it enjoyed a wealth of natural resources, good governance and an educated and skilled workforce. Sadly, its recent history has not been positive—today, Zimbabwe is burdened with deep economic, political and social troubles.

During the economic turmoil of 2005 to 2009 when hyperinflation stood at an alarming rate of 300 to 400 percent, less than 20 percent of the population was employed and more than half were relying on foreign food aid. Dollarization—the removal of Zimbabwean currency from circulation and the use of US dollars—put an end to hyperinflation in 2009, and has finally brought slow but real economic growth and some stability to the country. Although the economy of Zimbabwe has shown gradual signs of improvement, the political situation remains volatile and uncertain.

Even as inflation appears to be under control, the cost of living has escalated, making everyday items unaffordable for many. According to The Consumer Council for Zimbabwe, a typical food basket in 2013 costs US$159.33, as compared to US$142.77 in 2010. Besides essential items of food, other basic commodities such as fuel and transport costs have also risen. In 2013, the median monthly disposable salary after tax in Zimbabwe was US$500. Basic utilities cost an average of US$125 for electricity, gas, and water. The average costs for milk and bread are US$1.55 and US$1.50 respectively.

For over a decade, Zimbabwe has been considered by many to be a country in crisis and even a "failed state." This situation was partly triggered by the country's involvement in the war in the Democratic Republic of Congo as well as the chaotic and violent land seizures carried out by Mugabe supporters throughout most of the 2000s.

Ordinary Zimbabweans in every major town and city face numerous difficult challenges on a daily basis. In addition to their struggle just to make a living, many people have to endure and manage without the basics of life such as clean water, food, electricity, and sanitation. Everyday transactions are complicated by the fact that people have to procure foreign currencies, mostly US dollars, to pay for essential goods and services. During the period of fluctuating inflation, making even small purchases was arduous, as it required carrying large amounts of cash.

Due to a lack of investment and funding, the infrastructure of the country is under enormous strain; and the standard of public services has declined drastically. Both the healthcare and the education systems are fragile, even on the brink of collapse, and are unable to cope with the needs of its people.

In 2011, it was reported that there were only 1.7 hospital beds for every 1,000 patients and in 2007, only one physician was available to every 12,000 patients. Like many other African countries, Zimbabwe has an AIDS/HIV epidemic which has been exacerbated by poor healthcare, a lack of skilled health professionals, and food shortages. It is believed that 1.2 million people are living with HIV/AIDS, affecting 1 in 10 adults in the country. There are also 1 million children who have been orphaned as a consequence of this disease. Sadly, the current state of affairs in Zimbabwe's health system means it cannot easily provide the necessary care and medication for the sick.

Zimbabwe once enjoyed one of the best education and schooling systems in Africa. Its literacy rate has always been high and even now, over 83 percent of the population over the age of 15 years old can read and write English. Its political and economic problems have adversely affected the education of Zimbabwe's youth to such an extent that in 2008, the school year had to be cancelled mainly due to lack of public funds. In 2003, school life expectancy stood at only 9 years for girls and 10 years for boys.

As poverty becomes widespread, crime too becomes rife; and distrust and conflict continue to grow among people of different ethnic groups. Many today live in fear of violence and some live with a sense of disillusionment. Many are forced to live from hand to mouth and to take each day as it comes.

Life is hard for the majority of people in Zimbabwe and this is reflected in its life expectancy and infant mortality rates. Life expectancy is declining rapidly and according to the United Nations, it is one of the lowest in the world. The average life expectancy stands at 52 years. Infant mortality rate stands at 27 deaths for every 1000 live births.

Although there is no doubt that life is a daily struggle, Zimbabweans are a naturally entrepreneurial people and will try their utmost to eke out a living, however small. It seems as if on every corner in every town, city, and even along highways and roadsides, long lines of market stalls can be seen with traders selling all manner of things from milk, vegetables, bread, chickens, and household goods including cooking oil and soap. Many of these hardworking traders are women who use their meager income to buy food and keep their children at school.

Overcrowding in classrooms is a norm due to the lack of education facilities and teachers for the children.

Women and men hoe under the sun at a tobacco plantation. Workers have to brave the heat to produce crops, their source of income.

Life is also a challenge for the small minority of white farmers who have chosen to remain in Zimbabwe in spite of the violence against them. Many have stayed to protect their farms, which have been in their families for generations but which now have been forcibly invaded and taken away from them. Many white farmers have had to watch helplessly as looters plunder their crops and farming equipment. Some of these farmers have been viciously beaten and even killed, together with their families and farm workers. In 2010, only 400 white farmers were left in the country compared to 4500 in 2000. White Zimbabweans now make up less than 1 percent of the population of over 12 million.

Zimbabweans from all walks of life have had to and continue to endure varying degrees of police and military corruption and a general state of lawlessness. To add to its woes, Zimbabwe has also suffered from several disastrous droughts—one of the worst in 1992 but also more recently in 2012. This has badly affected food production and deepened the food crisis. In addition to its already critical problems, the international community imposed economic sanctions on Zimbabwe in 2002 to encourage its government to improve its human rights record. Since the coalition government formed in 2009, some of these sanctions have been lifted but not all. Many believe that these punitive sanctions have not worked and in fact, have brought more suffering to ordinary Zimbabweans.

Zimbabwean youth make up more than half of the population. At present, there is a high level of dissatisfaction among them as it is virtually impossible to secure a job with unemployment running at more than 90 percent. Thousands of talented young people graduate from universities and colleges every year hoping to find employment but only a fraction achieve it. Although the economy is growing, progress is being made at an extremely slow pace and people, young and old, continue to struggle to earn decent wages to support themselves and their families. It is dispiriting especially for young graduates to have to resort to working in menial jobs, but this is now common in Zimbabwe. The unemployment rate is high at about 80 percent and that of youths from ages 15 to 24 years stands at roughly 60 percent.

Apart from the youth, the women in Zimbabwe continue to bear heavy burdens as the country struggles to overcome its economic problems and political unrest. Women account for more than half the population but have little representation in politics and business. Ordinary women are unsurprisingly the victims of the economic crisis—many work tirelessly for very little money to feed and educate their children. Around 18 percent of women in Zimbabwe are HIV positive but access to healthcare is limited. In the sphere of education, women are also discriminated against as more girls than boys are made to leave school as families find themselves unable to afford the compulsory school fees. As fewer girls complete their education and gain qualifications, the majority remain trapped in poverty.

Millions of Zimbabweans who can have left this desperate state of affairs by moving to other countries, particularly to South Africa and the United Kingdom, where many live in exile. This has resulted in a severe "brain drain" of skilled workers who are much needed if Zimbabwe is to recover from the crisis it finds itself in today.

As Zimbabwe prepares for the future, President Robert Mugabe remains in power albeit in an uncomfortable power-sharing government with the opposition leader, Morgan Tsvangirai, who was sworn in as prime minister in February 2009. Tsvangirai has declared the coalition government as unworkable as he and his party believe that Mugabe has no regard for the coalition. There are constant rumors circulating that Mugabe suffers from deteriorating health. There is great uncertainty about what would follow after Mugabe's death as he has led the country for more than 30 years and, in spite of the criticisms against him, is regarded by many as a hero who liberated the nation from colonialist powers.

Many believe that as long as Mugabe remains in charge, Zimbabwe will not be able to start its journey to rebuild itself. It is feared that the new discovery of precious diamonds in 2006 in the Chiadzwa area has provided Mugabe and his supporters enough wealth to stay in power for a longer period of time.

In spite of the multitude of challenges, Zimbabweans are known for not giving up easily. They are generally a warm and fun-loving people who place great emphasis on family values and community. More importantly, they are a hopeful and optimistic people—qualities which they will need to help them regenerate their country.

GEOGRAPHY

An aerial view of the majestic Victoria Falls.

ZIMBABWE IS SITUATED on the south of the African continent. Covering 150,872 square miles (390,757 square km), Zimbabwe is about the size of California. It is boun.ded on all sides by land: South Africa to the south, Botswana to the southwest, Zambia to the north, and Mozambique to the east, separating Zimbabwe from the Indian Ocean.

Zimbabwe is blessed with natural resources that once helped make the nation one of Africa's most prosperous.

THE SHAPE OF ZIMBABWE

Much of Zimbabwe is part of the great plateau dominating Southern Africa. Shaped like a vast upside-down saucer, the plateau tilts upward toward the east, with areas of varying altitudes.

A high area known as the High Veld takes the form of a ridge that runs from the southwest to the northeast. This is the backbone of the country. Altitudes in this area do not fall below 4,000 feet (1,219 m) above sea level, making it ideal for cash-crop cultivation.

On each side of the High Veld lies the wider plateau of the Middle Veld, with an elevation between 2,000 and 4,000 feet (610 and 1,219 m). Toward the south the Low Veld rises 500 to 2,000 feet (152—610 m). It is hot and dry, a poor place for cultivation.

1

Zimbabwe boasts three National Parks—Mana Pools, Matobo, and Victoria Falls-which have been awarded UNESCO World Heritage status.

ROCK FORMATIONS   The undulating landscape of the High Veld is interrupted by intrusions of hard rock. A notable example of these formations is the Great Dike, 300 miles (483 km) long, 6 miles (10 km) wide. Formed by solidified magma resulting from volcanic activity 1.2 billion years ago, the Great Dike contains rich seams of chromite, asbestos, nickel, and platinum. Its mineral-rich content is one of the country's most valuable resources.

The Matopo Hills are another example of formations caused by these intrusions. However, the Matopo Hills are dwarfed by the mountainous Eastern Highlands, where Mount Nyangani (formerly know as Mount Inyangani), at 8,504 feet (2,592 m), rises as the highest mountain in Zimbabwe.

RIVERS

There are two main rivers in Zimbabwe: the Limpopo in the south and the Zambezi in the north. Both help to define the country's political borders. The Limpopo separates Zimbabwe from the Republic of South Africa, while the Zambezi marks the boundary with Zambia.

THE MATOPO HILLS

The Matopo Hills are located 310 miles (499 km) south of Victoria Falls, near the city of Bulawayo. The hills, formed of granite and gneiss, are known as kopjes and are millions of years old. Caves there were home to the earliest human inhabitants of Zimbabwe. On the walls of the caves are paintings that date back some 13,000 years.

In the first half of the 19th century the Ndebele migrated to the Matopo Hills from their Zulu homelands. The Ndebele regarded the hills and caves of the Matopo region as sacred. When their king Mzilikazi died, his remains were sealed in a hillside tomb. The Ndebele still hold spiritual ceremonies in the Matopo Hills. The area is also the burial site of Cecil John Rhodes, the leader and financier of the first white settlers of Zimbabwe.

Geographically the Matopo Hills are interesting for the unusual granite outcrops that characterize the area. Wind and water have eroded and shaped the isolated granite blocks into strange and wonderful formations that resemble animals and human faces. Some of the rocks are precariously balanced one on top of the other, while others lie scattered as if they had been thrown around by a mighty giant. Mzilikazi named the area "Matobos," meaning the "bald-headed ones," after the granite masses; the word was later corrupted to "Matopos."

The Zambezi river as seen from the Elephant Hills Resort.

ZAMBEZI The Zambezi flows for 2,200 miles (3,541 km), making it one of the longest rivers in Africa. After the Zambezi's dramatic 300-foot (91-m) drop into a mile-wide chasm at Victoria Falls, the river flows through the Kariba Gorge. There its waters are harnessed by a dam, forming the 2,000-square mile (5,180-square km) Lake Kariba. The enormous mass of water creates great pressure and feeds a power station that supplies electricity to Zimbabwe and Zambia.

LIMPOPO The Limpopo is 1,100 miles (1,770 km) long and flows north from South Africa, forming that country's borders with Botswana and Zimbabwe. Changes in the volume of the river affect people in nearby areas. A drought may dry up the river basin and reduce the water supply, while a cyclone may cause the basin to flood some areas.

Until tensions between South Africa and Zimbabwe relaxed in the 1990s, the section of the Limpopo between the two countries was filled with steel netting. This was to catch the floating mines that South Africa feared would be released by Black Nationalist guerrillas operating from Zimbabwe. The section of the river is still heavily guarded, though now it is to prevent jobless Zimbabweans from crossing into South Africa to work there.

Victoria Falls, situated on the Zambezi River, is described as one of the seven natural wonders of the world. More than 150 million years old, the falls were created at a time when volcanic lava from the earth's crust cooled and contracted, forming crevices. These crevices gradually expanded under the influence of the flooding of the Zambezi, resulting in a gorge. The gorge now receives a vast cascade of water from the Zambezi River as it tumbles into the chasm.

The tremendous power of the water falling 355 feet (108 m) creates a terrific roar that can be heard from a distance of 20 miles (32 km). In addition to the noise, clouds of spray rise into the air and create a mist that is visible nearly 4 miles (6 km) away. The African name for the falls is "Mosi-oa-tunya," which means the smoke that thunders.

David Livingstone, the 19th-century Scottish explorer and missionary, is often referred to as the person who discovered Victoria Falls. Livingstone first saw the falls in 1855 and named them in honor of Britain's Queen Victoria.

It is more accurate to credit Livingstone with being the first white person to see the falls, as he had been taken there by local Africans to view the spectacle. Livingstone's astonishment at the phenomenon, as he traveled along the Zambezi River, is recorded in his diary. He described the falls as being so impressive that they "must have been gazed on by angels in their flight."

CLIMATE

Zimbabwe's climate varies by altitude, with the low-lying areas being the hottest. October is the warmest month, when average temperature highs reach 86°F (30°C) on the Low Veld and 70°F (21°C) on the High Veld. The summer season lasts from September to April. Wintertime, from May to August, is coldest on the High Veld. Although the nights are cold, the days are usually warm and sunny.

The cooler temperatures on the High Veld, combined with regular rainfall, help produce an ideal climate for farming. The subtropical conditions provide a perfect environment for grass to grow tall and for raising cattle. The main towns in the High Veld, Harare and Bulawayo, receive an average of eight hours of sunshine every day throughout the year.

Rainfall is heaviest in the Eastern Highlands, where the monsoon winds cross from the Indian Ocean to meet the tall mountains. The winds are forced high into the sky, where they form heavy clouds of water droplets. The consequent rains help to water this part of the country, resulting in lush vegetation.

In the low-lying areas, the climate is dry and hot and not conducive to farming. The grass is coarse and only bush and thorny trees manage to prosper in the harsh and dry heat. The lack of rainfall means that growing crops on a commercial basis is often unprofitable. Nevertheless, there has been success in irrigating the Low Veld in the southeast. Land that was once suitable only for ranching is proving to be lucrative agriculturally.

VEGETATION

Much of Zimbabwe's terrain consists of grassland. There are evergreen forests in the east and savanna woodland in the west. Brachystegia, a tall hardwood, grows in the Middle Veld and the High Veld.

Many of Zimbabwe's most beautiful wildflowers grow in the Nyanga region in the Eastern Highlands. The flame lily, for example, the national flower of Zimbabwe, is a climbing vine with bright red flowers that bloom in summer.

One of the most famous trees in Zimbabwe, found in many parts of Africa, is the baobab tree. It grows in the drier areas of south and southwestern Zimbabwe. In times of drought, elephants eat the juicy wood beneath the bark of the baobab tree.

The baobab tree has a thick trunk and many branches that spread outward, sometimes with leaves, other times bare. Large white flowers bloom between October and December. The fiber of the bark of the tree can be used to make rope and cloth.

The baobab often lives for more than a thousand years. In the vicinity of Victoria Falls, there is a famous baobab tree that bears the signature of David Livingstone; it is reported to be more than a thousand years old.

The sausage tree, with its large gray-brown, sausage-shaped pods, is another interesting member of Zimbabwe's flora. The sausage fruit is inedible, but its leaves and deep red flowers are food for antelopes, baboons, bats, birds, and elephants.

FAUNA

A great diversity of animals lives in the wild and in parks and reserves in Zimbabwe. Elephants, hippopotamuses, and crocodiles abound. Lions and giraffes are also common.

Antelopes and zebras are favorite targets for hungry lions, although antelopes can often outrun a lion during a chase and zebras can deliver a fatal kick when attacked.

Aardvarks and zorillas, though far apart in the dictionary, live side by side in Zimbabwe. The aardvark eats insects. It uses its long and narrow snout to forage close to the ground and its donkey-like ears to detect sounds of danger. Like the aardvark, the zorilla, or African polecat, is a nocturnal creature. Its diet, however, is more varied. It feeds on small mammals, birds, and invertebrates. Like skunks, zorillas excrete a foul smell to repel predators.

Zimbabwe's venomous snakes include boomslangs, black-necked cobras, and mambas. The mamba is one of the world's most venomous snakes. There are four species: three green and one black. The black mamba moves very fast and will chase its prey before injecting it with a powerful nerve toxin. The green mambas are not as aggressive as the black species and will not usually attack mammals. They prefer lizards, eggs, and small birds.

ANTELOPES Zimbabwe is home to many species of antelopes, such as the impala, with its patches of black fur above its hoofs. The males have gently spiralling horns. The gnu, or wildebeest, travels in groups varying in size from a dozen to a few hundred.

A giraffe in Hwange National Park. While only two subspecies of this animal is currently endangered, factors like poaching and habitat loss continues to decrease its numbers.

HWANGE NATIONAL PARK

The largest national park in Zimbabwe is Hwange, covering nearly 6,000 square miles (15,540 square km) in the northwestern corner of the country. The next most important park is Mana Pools, some 260 miles (418 km) east of the capital, Harare, where the increasingly rare black rhinoceros is found.

The Hwange National Park is home to about 20,000 elephants, its number doubled in size in five years as a result of an end to culling. There are also other animals, including over 100 mammals and over 400 species of birds. The land itself forms the most easterly side of the vast Kalahari Desert that covers two-thirds of neighboring Botswana. The national park was formed in 1929 because no other use for the land could be found. Parts of it had formerly been an Ndebele hunting reserve. Today the only hunters are tourists who take part in controlled safari hunts. Quotas for trophy animals are set by a government department. Between August and October, visitors flock to Hwange National Park to watch the animals.

MANA POOLS NATIONAL PARK

Mana Pools National Park situated by the Zambezi River, is home to a wide range of mammals such as elephants, leopards, hyena, zebra, buffalo, monkeys, baboons, impala, and lions. More than 450 species of birds and aquatic wildlife including hippopotamus and crocodiles also live there. In the Shona language, the word "Mana" means "four" and this unique and beautiful National Park is named after its four large inland pools.

The kudu has light stripes and stands about 72 inches tall at the shoulder. The male has long corkscrew-like horns that can grow as long as 3 feet (0.9 m).

Klipspringers feed in family groups and warn one another with a shrill whistle if they sense a predator.

NATURAL LANDSCAPES

Apart from the highlands in the Eastern part of the country, most of Zimbabwe is generally flat. The highest mountain in the country is Inyangani, at 8,504 feet (2, 592 m), while the lowest point is found in the south of the

country where the Rundi and Save rivers meet at an altitude of 531 feet (162 m) above sea level.

The scenery changes from one area to the next. A drive across the country passes through a variety of natural landscapes such as plains, mountains, valleys, and forests.

In the Eastern Highlands, the mountains and valleys have an Alpine look, but the names of the ranges are unmistakably African: Inyanga, Umvukwe, Chimani-mani. Once a refuge for people fleeing danger, the highlands now attract vacationers seeking outdoor leisure pursuits such as fishing, hiking, and climbing.

TOWNSCAPES

Zimbabwe's cities, towns, and villages are remarkably tidy and well-groomed. Streets in downtown areas are usually wide, a legacy of the days when they were planned to enable an ox-and-wagon team to turn around. Trees and colorful flowers line the roads, and the towns' names are planted in foxgloves and marigolds in local parks.

HARARE   The capital of Zimbabwe was founded in 1890. Originally Salisbury, the capital's name was changed to Harare when Zimbabwe became independent in 1980.

Harare's metropolitan area population has exceeded 1.606 million and is still growing as more people migrate from the countryside to find employment there. However, there are not enough jobs for everyone, and the poor live in shanty dwellings. The broad streets of Harare are characteristic of most Zimbabwean towns. Because of the pleasant climate year-round, parks and open spaces are filled with flowers. Even the trees bordering the streets flower in the summer.

BULAWAYO The second largest city in Zimbabwe, Bulawayo, has a population of over 655,600. It is an important industrial center; the surrounding area is rich in mineral deposits, and there are a number of large mines.

The city also attracts a large number of tourists because of its transportation links with Victoria Falls and the national parks. Bulawayo has historical importance; it was the center of what was once called Matabeleland—homeland to the Ndebele people, the most significant ethnic group in Zimbabwe after the Shona people.

CHITUNGWIZA This city—also known as Chi Town—in the northeast was formed in 1978 out of a group of small settlements. It has grown into the third largest city in Zimbabwe and is home to close to 354,480 people. Not many of the residents of Chitungwiza work there; most of them travel to the capital, 15 miles (24 km) north, for work.

INTERNET LINKS

www.zimparks.org/

Official website of The Zimbabwe Parks and Wildlife Management Authority providing a unique interactive experience for visitors and tourists to learn about various aspects including an overview, conservation, and more.

www.travel.nationalgeographic.com/travel/countries/zimbabwe-guide/#

Official website of National Geographic Travel featuring a Zimbabwe Guide providing information about the country through maps, facts, and video.

www.victoriafalls-guide.net/zambezi-river.html

Website providing information about The Zambezi River, which flows through Zimbabwe.

HISTORY

The conical tower of the Great Zimbabwe ruins. A city said to be built by members of the Gokomere culture, was wholly made of stones stacked on top of each other without the use of mortar and was an established trading center.

2

Before gaining independence in 1980, Zimbabwe had been known by these names— Rhodesia, Southern Rhodesia, and Zimbabwe-Rhodesia.

EVIDENCE OF A DISTINCTIVE Stone Age culture in Zimbabwe goes back 500,000 years. The early peoples were hunters and gatherers. They later settled down in agricultural communities. The earliest non-Africans to arrive in the land between the Limpopo and Zambezi rivers were Muslim traders, who were active on the Eastern coast from the 10th century.

After the Arabs came the Portuguese, but it was the British in the 19th century who made a permanent impression. They expropriated the land and named it Rhodesia.

Only after years of violent struggle did the country return to African rule. In 1980 Rhodesia was renamed Zimbabwe, after the ancient ruins, found about 19 miles (30 km) outside Masvingo (formerly Fort Victoria).

EARLY HISTORY

Most scholars believe that Africa was the birthplace of the human race. Stone tools and weapons such as hammers and spearheads have been discovered in Africa that date back some 2 million years. Early people in Zimbabwe also used the pigments from the iron in basalt rock to paint pictures, in shades of yellow, red, and brown, in caves. These ancient paintings are still well preserved.

It is thought that the San, or Bushmen, who still live in the Kalahari Desert of South Africa, are the descendants of the original inhabitants of southern and central Africa. The early San were driven into the desert by Bantu-speaking peoples when they migrated to this region.

GREAT ZIMBABWE

Archaeological evidence dates the arrival of an early Bantu culture in Zimbabwe around A.D. 300. The imposing stone structures of Great Zimbabwe were built by a Bantu-speaking people known as Shona, between the 12th and 15th centuries.

The structures are made up of three sections: the Hill Complex, the Valley Complex, and the Great Enclosure. They are the largest and most important constructions made by humans in Southern Africa before modern times. Early settlers from the West thought that the structures had been built by the ancient Egyptians or Phoenicians rather than by Africans in the area.

The Shona word "zimbabwe" translates as "stone houses." More than 200 stone structures were erected as the residences and power bases of the local kings and their representatives.

The Hill Complex is a steep 328-foot-high (100-m-high) granite hill dotted with ruins. A walled space near the summit may have been the king's headquarters or the seat of a royal spirit medium. The space contained stone bird figures, which were plundered by Europeans at the end of the 19th century. The Shona believed that the spiritual advisers to the king could communicate with their ancestors through the cries of the birds represented by the stone figures.

The Great Enclosure is a massive elliptical structure 36 feet (11 m) in height and 820 feet (250 m) in circumference. Thought to be the king's palace, the Great Enclosure contains a conical tower, the purpose and meaning of which remain unknown.

The Valley Complex has several ruins, indicating that the area was the social and political capital of Zimbabwe during the 14th and 15th centuries. Evidence of gold smelting, and an elaborate drainage system point to a prosperous community, which had a sophisticated trading network. Gold and copper from more than a thousand mines were exported through Mozambique to the coast to be shipped across the Indian Ocean. Manufactured goods were imported.

Centuries later, gold was found in some of Great Zimbabwe's ruins. A group of early European looters even founded a company called the Rhodesian Ancient Ruins Company.

Today Great Zimbabwe remains remarkable and impressive. It is the country's most popular tourist attraction after Victoria Falls. The ruins are the remains of a medieval African civilization that had a capital city of 10,000 people and that extended over most of what is Zimbabwe today.

MWENE MUTAPA

Sometime in the latter half of the 15th century, Great Zimbabwe was abandoned, and the seat of royal power moved north to a site on the Zambezi River. The reigning king, Nyatsimba, set about conquering the neighboring lands. In the process, he earned the title Mwene Mutapa, or Ravager of the Lands.

Mwene Mutapa became the name of an empire that was to rule until the 17th century. In the 16th century, the Portuguese moved in from the east and began exploring Mwene Mutapa land. They thought that the name of the empire was Monomotapa, and that was the name that entered the historical records.

An early attempt by the Portuguese to invade the country failed, but in 1630, they were able to install their own puppet king in the north of the country. The Portuguese ruled a large part of the country through force, and the people of Mwene Mutapa were unsuccessful in all their attempts to drive out the Portuguese.

A more independent spirit prevailed in the south of the country. The Rozwi dynasty controlled the region and built impressive structures near the present-day city of Bulawayo. In 1663 the Rozwi formed an alliance with Mwene Mutapa and defeated the Portuguese. Although the Portuguese no longer ruled the country, they maintained a trading presence. It would be some 300 years before the British arrived. In the meantime, Zimbabwe became home to a new group of Africans from the south, the Ndebele.

THE NDEBELE

The Ndebele, today concentrated in southwestern Zimbabwe, arrived in the first half of the 19th century. Until then, the Shona had lived throughout Zimbabwe. Apart from conflicts with the Portuguese, the Shona way of life had continued undisturbed for centuries. Meanwhile, to the south, in what is today South Africa, the rise of the Zulu warrior—Shaka—was to have a profound effect on Zimbabwe.

As Shaka's army grew in power and influence, Zulu clans were forced to accept his authority or flee. The shortage of land, made worse as white settlers moved into South Africa, added to the pressure to move. One of Shaka's warriors, Mzilikazi, fled with his people in 1823. In 1840, after attempting to settle in several places, they finally established a community in Zimbabwe.

The group, called Ndebele, were forced at first to survive by raiding cattle from neighboring settlements. Despite being surrounded by the dominant Shona, the Ndebele established their own cultural identity. They grew in number and eventually were able to subdue neighboring Shona clans.

The warlike Ndebele established a tax system and carried out plundering expeditions on the Shona. In return for cattle and women, the Ndebele offered the protection of their professional army. By 1870, when Lobengula became their new king, the Ndebele had become a permanent, powerful force of cattle farmers and warriors.

Ndebele influence extended well beyond their capital at Bulawayo. Anyone attempting to move into Zimbabwe had to negotiate a treaty or defeat Lobengula's army. This fact soon became obvious to the white adventurers, who were irresistibly drawn to Zimbabwe by stories of its countless gold mines.

CECIL RHODES

For nearly a century, Zimbabwe was known to the world as Rhodesia, after Cecil Rhodes, an Englishman who worked with great zeal to bring to the Africans what he believed to be the greatest civilization on Earth. His ambition

LOBENGULA

In the 19th century, whenever foreigners wanted to mine for gold in Zimbabwe, they went to Lobengula, the undisputed king of the land. Lobengula was no fool. He saw the greed of the white entrepreneurs who were so interested in his kingdom and did his best to contain their ambitions.

In 1888 Cecil Rhodes managed to secure an exclusive treaty with Lobengula through John Moffat, the son of the famous missionary Robert Moffat. In the early stages of negotiations, Lobengula was under the impression that no more than 10 Europeans would mine in his land at any time and that they would be subject to the law and authority of the Ndebele people.

However, the conditions that Lobengula expected never found their way onto paper, and Lobengula unknowingly signed away some of his people's valuable rights. He was tricked into granting a concession allowing the Europeans access to all the minerals in the "kingdom, principalities and domains, together with full power to do all things that they may deem necessary to win and procure same."

When Lobengula found out exactly what he had agreed to, he tried to cancel the agreement, but it was too late. Rhodes had persuaded the British government to give the

British South Africa Company the right to enter the country and undertake business there. By 1900 the British South Africa Company had established complete control in the new territory.

After three years, it was clear that the foreigners intended to make Ndebele land their home. Lobengula came under pressure from his own people to fight. He knew that his people's spears were no match for the guns of the Europeans, but Lobengula had to enter into battle to protect his people's land.

Soon the Ndebele were forced to set Bulawayo on fire and flee. Lobengula died some time later.

was to paint the map red—it was the practice of mapmakers to mark in red parts of the world that were part of the British Empire. He also wanted to build a railroad from the tip of South Africa to Northern Egypt.

At age 17 Rhodes left his home in England to join his brother on a cotton farm in Natal, South Africa. He later made his fortune by buying the rights to diamond fields in Kimberly. In a few years, he had amassed the rights to 90 percent of the world's diamonds.

Hearing the tales of adventurers about large reserves of gold in the land across the Limpopo River, Rhodes then set his sights on Zimbabwe. In 1890 he organized a group of 200 men who crossed the Limpopo and claimed the land that became Fort Victoria. His actions were justified on the grounds of the Rudd concession, negotiated with Lobengula, giving the British South Africa Company the right to mine in this area.

Rhodes's name lives on, no longer in the name of a country, but in the scholarships he established at Oxford University.

Cecil Rhodes also founded De Beers in 1888, a family of companies specializing in the mining and trading of diamonds to a worldwide market.

THE 1890 INVASION

The Pioneer Column, the group that Rhodes organized to cross the Limpopo River and march into Southern Zimbabwe, consisted of 200 prospectors, supported by 500 armed policemen. The prospectors were each promised 15 gold-prospecting claims and 3,000 acres (1,200 hectares) of land.

Having crossed the Limpopo, the column established Fort Victoria, the oldest town in Zimbabwe today. The column continued their journey east of Lobengula's territory. Soon, they came to rest near a hill that was once the domain of a local chief named Harare. The prospectors raised the Union Jack and called the place Fort Salisbury, after their prime minister.

The Shona accepted the presence of the British and even appealed to them for protection against Ndebele warriors. The Ndebele, however, were in constant conflict with the British. A boundary line was soon drawn between the land of the Ndebele and that of the Shona.

When Lobengula was defeated in 1893, the Ndebele lands were appropriated, and Mwene Mutapa and Rozwi lands became known as Rhodesia.

THE FIRST CHIMURENGA

In 1896 the Ndebele rose in revolt against the invaders. They were joined by the Shona, who had also been forced to give up land to prospectors who had found that the supply of gold was not enough to make them their fortunes. The rebellion was later called the First Chimurenga (chim-oo-RENG-ah). Roughly translated from Shona, the word "chimurenga" means "war of liberation."

Rhodes was able to use Western technology to his advantage. The handcranked Gatling and fully automatic Maxim machine guns were powerful weapons at the time. Cannons were also used to defeat the insurgents. When the rebels took refuge in caves, dynamite was used to force them out.

Later, Rhodes made peace with the Ndebele induna (in-DOO-nah), or headmen, with a promise to return occupied land. Left to fight on by themselves, the Shona people were systematically defeated and their leaders executed.

Before the First Chimurenga, the Ndebele and Shona peoples had around 300,000 head of cattle. Afterward, they were left with less than 15,000, as the prospectors had taken what they thought were Lobengula's. In fact the cattle belonged to the whole community. This was a great loss to the Ndebele and the Shona, because cattle were not only a means of livelihood, but a symbol of prestige as well.

THE SEEDS OF REVOLUTION

The British South Africa Company ran Rhodesia until the 1920s. In 1923 Rhodesia became Southern Rhodesia, a self-governing colony of the British Empire. This made no difference to most Africans, since the right to vote was based on British citizenship.

THE RHODES COLOSSUS
STRIDING FROM CAPE TOWN TO CAIRO.

A cartoon in 1892 features Rhodes's hold over Africa. The success of the *indaba*, or peace conference, held between the white settlers along with Ndebele leaders, sealed the British's hold over the country.

The traditional communal farming economy of the Africans was destroyed when the Europeans began amassing large tracts of land for their farms. Dispossessed Africans were employed as cheap labor or left to try to farm infertile land. Africans could not change their place of work without permission from their employers, and laws requiring Africans to carry passes made it easy to control the local population.

After World War II, large numbers of Europeans were attracted to Zimbabwe by the idea of making a prosperous living out of farming. The situation for the Africans deteriorated as the European population increased. New laws further dispossessed the African population of their ancestors' land.

The years after World War II saw the growth of nationalist aspirations, not only in Rhodesia but all across Africa. Despite strong opposition from nationalists, in 1953 a federation was formed between Southern Rhodesia (Zimbabwe), Northern Rhodesia (Zambia), and Nyasaland (Malawi). In 1963 the federation was dissolved, with Northern Rhodesia and Nyasaland only months from independence. In Southern Rhodesia, however, the European population dug their heels in, resisting calls for liberalization.

AFRICAN NATIONALISM

African nationalism in Southern Rhodesia made itself felt in the 1950s when a bus boycott against fare increases was organized in the capitol. In 1957 the African National Congress (ANC) was formed, calling for "the national unity of all inhabitants of this country in true partnership regardless of race, color, and creed." People held strikes and marches, leading to a ban on the ANC.

The repression intensified the fight for independence from minority rule. Opposition spread across the cities, and the army responded to a strike in Bulawayo by killing 18 demonstrators.

In 1961 the Zimbabwe African People's Union (ZAPU) was formed. Joshua Nkomo became its leader. A couple of years later, the Zimbabwe African National Union (ZANU) was formed. A leading member of ZANU was Robert Mugabe.

UNILATERAL DECLARATION OF INDEPENDENCE

As many parts of Africa gained independence from colonial rule, the British rulers became alarmed at the prospect of losing their power and privileges in Rhodesia. In 1965, after inconclusive discussions with the British government over African rule in Rhodesia, the Rhodesian prime minister, Ian Douglas

The Unilateral Declaration of Independence was signed in 1965, proclaiming Rhodesia's independence from the United Kingdom.

Smith, signed a Unilateral Declaration of Independence announcing the country's refusal to be bound by Britain.

The declaration stated, without agreement from Britain, that from November 11, 1965, the day the declaration was signed; Rhodesia would have complete authority over its own affairs. Britain did not recognize the declaration and stopped all trade with Rhodesia. The next year, the United Nations imposed economic sanctions on Rhodesia.

Amid problems arising from international sanctions and African nationalism, in 1970 the white minority government declared Rhodesia a republic. Britain and other countries did not recognize the government and constitution of the Rhodesian republic.

At the same time, the black majority was not happy about being governed by the white minority. Nationalist sentiments grew stronger, and in 1972 the Second Chimurenga broke out. Nationalist guerrillas trained in Zambia fought to liberate the country from white dominance. Numerous attacks were launched on Rhodesian security forces. As the guerrillas won the respect and understanding of the rural communities, government forces found it difficult to suppress the armed resistance.

Finally, in 1980, the Lancaster House Agreement led to the start of Rhodesia's transition from a British colony to the independent nation of Zimbabwe. A new prime minister, Robert Mugabe, was elected, and a new constitution was approved.

TIME FOR CHANGE

Despite popular discontent over the uneven distribution of land—with the white minority owning most of it—and government corruption, Mugabe continued to win elections throughout the 1980s and 1990s. In 1987 he became president, and his party, ZANU, merged with Joshua Nkomo's ZAPU opposition party to form the Zimbabwe African National Union Patriotic Front (ZANU-PF).

In the late 1990s, amid growing economic problems, people began protesting the high tax rates and veterans of the war for independence demanded compensation. In 2000, despite international opposition, the

Mugabe government seized white-owned farms and gave the land to the war veterans. This also caused disruptions to agricultural work and worsened economic problems in the country.

As Zimbabwe dealt with high inflation rates and food shortages, opposition toward Mugabe's leadership intensified. In 1999 a new opposition party, the Movement for Democratic Change (MDC), posed a serious threat to ZANU-PF. In 2002, although the MDC performed well at the elections, Mugabe managed to hold on to power amidst widespread evidence of electoral fraud. In 2005, the ruling ZANU-PF party won a majority of seats in the newly-created Senate. The opposition became split on whether to boycott the poll. Ordinary Zimbabweans continued to protest and riot against hyperinflation and a food crisis in the period from 2005 to 2009. In 2008, Mugabe and the leader of the opposition, Morgan Tsvangirai signed a power-sharing agreement with the latter being sworn in as Prime Minister in 2009. By 2011, both declared the power-sharing government as unworkable.

"I don't believe in majority rule ever in Rhodesia, not in a thousand years."
—Ian Smith, 1976

INTERNET LINKS

http://news.bbc.co.uk/1/hi/special_report/1998/12/98/zimbabwe/226542.stm

Official website of BBC News Online providing an at-a-glance guide to some of the key events and key dates in Zimbabwe's history.

www.historyworld.net/wrldhis/PlainTextHistories.asp?historyid=ad28

Official website of History World providing information about different eras in Zimbabwe's history from the Ndebele kingdom to the 2008 elections.

www.zimembassy.se/history.html

Official website of Stockholm's Embassy of Zimbabwe providing a useful short history of Zimbabwe.

GOVERNMENT

The courthouse in Bulawayo, Zimbabwe's second largest city.

3

I N THE EARLY YEARS after independence from white-minority rule, nearly a quarter of the white population fled, fearing an impending dictatorship. A fairly democratic state emerged instead, but in the 1990s, as Mugabe's determination to hold on to power at all costs became increasingly obvious, fears of a dictatorship materialized among many of Zimbabwe's black citizens as well.

Zimbabwean's Guards of Honor march during veteran leader Robert Mugabe's swearing-in ceremony in Harare on August 22, 2013.

In 1999 opposition groups began campaigning for changes in the country's constitution that would strengthen democratic rule. Mugabe, however, wanted to change the constitution to strengthen his political control. At the same time, the Movement for Democratic Change (MDC) emerged as the voice of opposition to ZANU-PF.

In 2000, when Mugabe lost a referendum, some 55 percent of the electorate voted to reject the government's revised constitution. The people campaigned for a constitutional change to limit the president's powers and time in office. The Mugabe government amended the constitution to legitimize the seizure of white-owned farms.

Mugabe's efforts to stay in power have included opposition bullying and vote rigging. The MDC party has won a number of by-elections, in which it has faced violent opposition from government supporters. Foreign journalists have also been expelled for reporting on illegal activities by the Mugabe government.

Anti-Mugabe protestors in Johannesburg, South Africa, carry posters outside the United Nationals World Summit for Sustainable Development in 2002 where Mugabe was to justify the controversial forced eviction of white farmers from their land.

SYSTEM OF GOVERNMENT

In theory, Zimbabwe is a parliamentary democracy with a constitution guaranteeing individual freedom, regardless of race, religion, or gender. In practice, Zimbabwe is a dictatorship that abuses its constitution.

The parliament consists of a House of Assembly with 150 members. Constitutional changes are supposed to have the support of two-thirds of the members of the Assembly.

The most powerful political position is that of the president. There is no limit to the number of consecutive terms the president can serve.

A new constitution is likely to emerge, but not before the country achieves some balance in political and economic power. The land issue lies behind much of the political wrangling in Zimbabwe's government. Countries such as South Africa have made attempts to mediate Zimbabwe's political and economic crisis. However, until the land issue is resolved, it is unlikely that a new and lasting constitution, followed by political and economic stability, will emerge. In 2012, the coalition government worked on drafting a new constitution for Zimbabwe.

DEMOCRACY OR DICTATORSHIP?

Even though it cannot be denied that Zimbabwe has experienced fair amount of constitutional rule in comparison to other African countries, in the present the government is essentially acting as a one-party state.

SIGNS OF DEMOCRACY For seven years, ZANU allowed 20 seats in the parliament for whites, when their minority status would hardly have justified more than one or two seats.

Zimbabwe is a one-party state, but opposition parties are allowed. The Movement for Democratic Change (MDC) has contested elections, claiming that the elections were rigged.

Compared to the rest of Africa, Zimbabwe has a good record of constitutional rule. Signs of an independent press can be seen in the newspaper's allegations of government corruption. The University of Zimbabwe has also been a source of strident anti-government criticism. The university has been closed down from time to time because of this, but it continues to flourish.

SIGNS OF DICTATORSHIP Although forced into a power-sharing government with the opposition in 2008, ZANU-PF is committed to a one-party state, leaving no alternative for voters during elections. In the period of unrest following independence, there were serious allegations of mistreatment, and in some cases murder, of the Ndebele minority. The government does not allow organizations such as Amnesty International to investigate human rights violations in Zimbabwe. Television and radio are owned and controlled by the government.

The Emergency Powers Act gives the government the right to act in a way that is undemocratic in cases that it considers to be emergencies. When the former Prime Minister Abel Muzorewa spoke out against the ZANU government, he was jailed on charges of subversion.

Robert Mugabe, former Prime Minister and current President of Zimbabwe.

ROBERT MUGABE

Robert Mugabe was imprisoned in 1964 for 10 years by the white-minority government of the country in which he now serves as president. Born in 1924, he received six years' elementary education in a mission school. Later, he studied for two years to become a teacher. During his years in prison, he studied law and finished six college degrees. After his release, he left the then Rhodesia and fought a guerrilla war against the government. In 1979, he was instrumental in the Lancaster House negotiations which finally gave Zimbabwe its independence. In 1987, he assumed the position of President of Zimbabwe.

HIS SUCCESSES Mugabe became the leader of ZANU-PF because of his radical opposition to white-minority rule and his unwillingness to compromise on the issue of black-majority rule. He was portrayed in the media as a monster and the country's number-one public enemy. When ZANU-PF won in the 1980 elections and Mugabe became the leader of the country, the black community celebrated in the streets, although there was apprehension among the white population.

In time, Mugabe convinced the whites that they had nothing to fear and won their respect. But there was opposition from the Ndebele minority. It took nearly 10 years of bloodshed and the loss of countless lives for Mugabe to merge the Ndebele with the new Zimbabwe. In spite of the economic, social and political turmoil, many believe he has brought upon Zimbabwe, Mugabe continues to prove that he is a survivor. In 2011, Mugabe announced that he would run in the next elections.

General elections were held in Zimbabwe in July 2013. Mugabe was re-elected with ZANU-PF winning a two-thirds majority in the House of Assembly.

HIS FAILURES Although Mugabe won landslide election victories in the 1990s, his popularity soon began to decline very quickly. His failure to solve basic economic problems concerning economic growth and the creation of sustained employment resulted in bread riots and severe fuel shortages. In 2005, the UN declared that Zimbabwe was "in meltdown" and the US labelled the country "an outpost of tyranny."

The land issue remains a controversial policy that has lost Zimbabwe a lot of international respect. International investors are dissuaded from investing in a country where the government seizes economic resources for political reasons.

Zimbabwe's political and economic situation today raises the probability that Mugabe would finally relinquish his grip on power after more than 30 years of rule, leaving the country to grapple with the question of whom to elect in his place and how to do so democratically.

THE OPPOSITION

The main opposition party to ZANU-PF is the multi-ethnic MDC. The MDC was formed in 1999 by a group of about 700 people from various backgrounds who came together to find solutions to the everyday struggles of ordinary Zimbabweans such as their struggle for employment, food, equal rights, and justice. In 2000, the party held its inaugural congress and Morgan Tsvangirai

"The government has seriously failed and the people are now saying, 'Enough is enough!'"
—The MDC mayor of Harare, June 2003.

became its President. Led by Tsvangirai, the MDC almost succeeded in gaining a victory over Zanu-PF in the parliamentary elections in 2000.

In 2002 and 2003, Morgan Tsvangirai was charged with two counts of treason including an allegation to kill President Mugabe, but he was acquitted in 2004 and 2005. Amidst MDC's claims that the ruling Zanu-PF's victory in the 2005 election was rigged; the party became split over the decision to boycott the poll.

In 2007, Morgan Tsvangirai was hospitalized after his arrest at a rally where one man was shot dead by riot police. In the 2008 presidential and parliamentary elections, the opposition MDC claimed victory but the electoral body declared that the victory was not enough to avoid a run-off against Mugabe who was declared the winner, resulting in Tsvangirai withdrawing from the polls.

Later in 2008, Mugabe and Tsvangirai signed a historic power-sharing agreement. In 2009, Tsvangirai was sworn in as prime minister, following difficult discussions over the establishment of government.

In 2009, Tsvangirai suffered a personal tragedy where he was injured but sadly, his wife was killed in a car crash. In 2011, two years after agreeing to the power-sharing deal, MDC declared the deal unworkable as a result of Zanu-PF's violent disregard for democracy.

Morgan Tsvangirai, Zimbabwe's Prime minister and leader of the Movement for Democratic Change (MDC) addresses an election campaign rally at Mkoba Stadium in Gweru in July 2013.

Despite having put up a good fight in numerous national elections over the years, the MDC party has not been able to topple the ZANU-PF party. Nevertheless, on the local level, the MDC party has had several victories. Zimbabwe has eight provinces (Manicaland, Mashonaland Central, Mashonaland East, Mashonaland West, Masvingo, Matabeleland North, Matabeleland South, and Midlands) and two cities recognized as provinces (Harare and Bulawayo). Each province is run by its own local government.

In 2012, the MDC continued to campaign for democracy in Zimbabwe by officially complaining that its election rallies were being stopped and highlighted that police and political violence are on the increase.

In August 2013, the MDC tried to have the presidential election results declared null and void in protest of Mugabe's re-election. However, they withdrew their petition a week later.

INTERNET LINKS

www.zim.gov.zw/

Official website of the Zimbabwean government providing information on The Premier, Ministries, Departments, Judiciary, Parliament and more.

www.mdc.co.zw/

Official website of Zimbabwe's main opposition political party — the Movement for Democratic Change with information about the party, its leader and agenda.

www.zimbabwedemocracynow.com/

Website of Zimbabwe Democracy Now with information on its various campaigns, press releases, and opinions.

www.zimbabwesituation.com/

Online daily updates on news and politics in Zimbabwe today with news archives and links to other news websites.

ECONOMY

Women harvest chilies at a farm. Efforts have been made to create sustainable tabasco chili farming through an irrigation scheme, which uses water from a nearby river to support growth.

ZIMBABWE HAS A WEALTH of natural resources, with large deposits of valuable minerals lying near fertile agricultural lands. Blessed with a farm-friendly climate, Zimbabwean land is usually able to support a wide variety of crops.

Wheat, barley, oats, millet, soybeans, and groundnuts are all produced on a commercial basis. Tobacco is a valuable crop, although sugar, tea, and coffee are also important. There were also large farms devoted to raising livestock: cattle, pigs, and sheep.

Once known as "the bread basket of Southern Africa," the country usually produced more than enough agriculturally to feed itself. However, in recent years, due to the political and economic crisis, Zimbabwe has experienced severe food shortages and struggles to feed its own people.

The main economic problems in Zimbabwe stem from the poor distribution and use of fertile land. More than half of all Zimbabweans—about 66 percent—earn a living directly from agriculture, but less than 11 percent of the country's arable land is being cultivated, and people do not have equal access to the country's rich agricultural resources.

Unequal land ownership, a major concern of the government of independent Zimbabwe, is a legacy of the nation's colonial history. When the colonialists turned to agriculture to obtain profits, they took large tracts of land away from the local farmers, who were sent to remote areas where they had to work under harsh conditions in order to earn a meager living.

In the past, most of the country's most fertile land remained in the hands of a small section of the population—the big commercial

4

Previously one of the strongest in Africa, Zimbabwe's economy since 2000 has suffered desperately. However, there are now gradual signs of growth.

farmers. Farming families in the rural areas cultivated the remaining, less fertile land but their plots did not produce enough to support their families. Even after Mugabe's land reform, Zimbabwe's agricultural sector remains fragile. In 2011, a large proportion of previously commercially farmed land sits overgrown or is only used for subsistence farming. Poverty affects almost three-quarters of the Zimbabwean population and 30 percent of the population is considered malnourished.

THE LEGACY OF RACISM

When Zimbabwe gained independence from Britain in 1980, a third of its arable land belonged to a white minority that made up just 1 percent of the population. The white farmers had tremendous economic power, because their land produced nearly half of the country's annual income in exports.

Mugabe and his party launched the land reform program in 1979, and promised to resettle more than 150,000 black families on white-owned land. Initially, the government bought land from white farmers, but land reform proceeded very slowly. In 1990 the government began taking over white-owned farms, compensating the owners with government bonds. That triggered international criticism and reduced foreign investment. From 2000, the Fast Track Resettlement Program was launched and black farmers began to seize and occupy farms owned by whites, often violently.

The land issue remains unresolved and controversial. Thousands of black families have so far been resettled, but many Zimbabweans are still trying to make a living from land that they have been resettled on. There is a pressing need to resettle them in areas better suited for cultivation. Their land is often overpopulated and overcultivated, resulting in problems such as deforestation and soil erosion. Irregular rainfall can cause serious droughts, as in early 1992 when a drought reached crisis proportions. People's lives were at risk, and the country had to look to other countries for food supplies.

The crisis over the seizure of white-owned farms added to the country's economic woes. The consequences of this crisis combined with poor rainfall resulted in 45 percent of the corn crop, the basic food crop, failing in 2012.

In January 2013, the government ceased seizure of foreign-owned farms protected by bilateral investment agreements after a group of 40 Dutch farmers won a lawsuit for the loss of their land.

TOBACCO FARMING

Tobacco used to be one of Zimbabwe's most valuable products. More than a half million people worked on tobacco farms in the country. Tobacco was the country's biggest foreign currency earner. However, as a result of the political crisis, all exports, including the export of tobacco crops, have been impacted. In 2001, Zimbabwe was the world's sixth largest producer of tobacco. Today, it produces significantly less—in the decade between 2000 to 2010, tobacco productions fell by more than 40 percent.

Zimbabwean tobacco is of high quality. Most of it used to be exported to European countries. On tobacco farms, seedlings are planted in November to catch the rainfall at that time of the year. The seedlings require plenty of water, but the soil must also be well-drained in order for them to thrive.

There is a moral issue involved in the production of tobacco for the manufacture of cigarettes because of the harmful effects of smoking on health. One way Zimbabwe could respond to criticism about its social responsibility as a major global tobacco producer is to find other uses for tobacco that do not endanger the health of the consumer.

RICH DIVERSITY

There is far more to Zimbabwe's agricultural economy than just tobacco and corn farming. Other agriculture products include cotton, wheat, coffee, sugarcane, peanuts, sheep, goats, and pigs.

Tobacco being auctioned in Harare. The agriculture industry is once again looking up as more international buyers have been flocking to the auction floors to buy bales of tobacco. Interestingly, a majority of black farmers have been harvesting the product in recent years, compared to white farmers in past.

Softwoods such as pine and eucalyptus are grown commercially, especially in the Eastern Highlands. Zimbabwe has some of the world's tallest eucalyptus trees, which originally came from Australia.

Tea is farmed intensively, and Zimbabwe is self-sufficient in the crop. Coffee plantations are on the increase. Zimbabwe's Tanganda Tea is one of the largest grower and producer of both tea and coffee in all of Africa. Hops are also grown to produce Zimbabwe's lager beer, which have been exported to countries such as the United States. In the 1940s, some farmers established vineyards to meet the demand for wine in the absence of imports. Today Zimbabwe produces some quality white wine.

Raising cattle for the export of beef was introduced by the white settlers. It was an important part of the economy. To black farmers, cattle signify power and prestige, but today, they lack capital and good grazing land to raise cattle on a commercial scale.

INDUSTRY

Most of Zimbabwe's minerals are exported, while the rest provide the country with the raw materials for its industries. The Great Dike has reserves of platinum and chromite that will provide a secure future for mining in the country long after the reserves of copper and nickel have been depleted.

The Iron and Steel Corporation used to be the largest steelworks in Zimbabwe, which employed thousands of people, making it one of the largest employers of industrial workers. The company produces a variety of metal products for use in manufacturing everything from plowshares to components for locomotive engines. It has faced many problems recently, but in 2011 it received much-needed foreign investment which is being used to revive the corporation's fortunes.

Zimbabwe's power industry includes the massive Kariba Dam, which it shares with Zambia, on the Zambezi River. The construction of new hydroelectric plants along Zimbabwe's rivers will add enormously to the country's ability to meet its energy needs.

Most of Zimbabwe's industry is located in the vicinity of the two main centers of population, Harare and Bulawayo. Both have vital railroad connections. In the Eastern part of the country, where important timber plantations are located, the town of Mutare (moo-TAR-ay) is a hub of commercial activity, largely due to its strategic road link with the busy Mozambique port of Beira on the eastern coast of Africa. Sadly, the timber industry has been badly affected by a combination of illegal settlement and forest fires as a result of the political chaos in the country.

MINING

Mining is the oldest industry in Zimbabwe, dating back thousands of years to the Iron Age. Burial sites of Iron Age nobility that have been excavated reveal a sophisticated use of gold. Some of the finds include seashells set in gold and delicate necklaces of twisted gold. However, perhaps due to its abundance, gold was not worshiped as the ultimate mineral. Jewelry crafted from iron was just as highly regarded.

Nevertheless, it was gold that attracted the attention of the Arab traders, Portuguese navigators, and British entrepreneurs. The British thought that so many gold mines promised equally abundant profits, but many of the mines they tried to exploit had already been worked dry and the ones that were still mineworthy often did not repay the investment in machinery. Then a gold prospector discovered coal near Victoria Falls, and that started a profitable coal industry that is still important to Zimbabwe's economy.

Apart from gold and coal, Zimbabwe is also rich in other valuable minerals. In the 1950s emeralds were discovered and 10 years later enormous nickel reserves. The 1970s brought a bigger surprise—the discovery of platinum. A modern plant opened in 1992, supplied by the world's largest reserve of platinum outside South Africa. Some 60 metal and minerals, including chromium, cobalt, copper, iron, silver, and tin, are mined in Zimbabwe.

While many countries in Africa have become dependent on a core natural resource, such as oil in Nigeria or copper in Zambia, Zimbabwe relies on several, which makes it relatively resilient to fluctuations in commodity prices. For example, when the price of asbestos fell due to concerns about its effect on health and the environment, Zimbabwe did not suffer catastrophic consequences for its annual production.

Today, the mining industry contributes about 13 percent to Zimbabwe's GDP. Its most valuable minerals include gold, asbestos, chromite, coal, and base metals.

DIAMONDS

Another of Zimbabwe's valuable minerals includes the diamonds that are found in the Marange diamond fields, which in 2010, was declared the world's biggest diamond find in over a century. Originally owned by the prestigious De Beers company, the Zimbabwean government took over ownership in 2006. In the same year, a diamond rush began where thousands of illegal workers began mining small plots at Marange, causing a black market to develop.

Diamond mining in Zimbabwe is highly controversial as it has been the subject of allegations of human rights abuses by the military and police and illegal money laundering by Mugabe supporters. Zimbabwe is a participant in the Kimberley Process that regulates trade in diamonds. Since 2007, the Kimberley Process has voiced its concerns over human rights abuses in the diamond mining industry, threatening to suspend Zimbabwe from its certification program. However, the Kimberley Process has decided to work with Zimbabwe and in 2010, Zimbabwe was permitted to resume the sale of diamonds from the Marange fields. Those who oppose the decision to allow Zimbabwe to gain financially from its diamond industry despite serious allegations of torture and human rights abuses, call these diamonds "blood diamonds."

HYPERINFALTION YEARS

In the five-year period between 2004 to 2009, Zimbabwe experienced a state of hyperinflation—at one stage, the annual rate of price growth reached beyond 11 million percent. The situation was made worse by the government

A gold processing plant for crushing and separating ore for metal extraction in Zimbabwe. Gold production has been more than halved compared to when it was at its peak over 10 years ago, due to poor production capacity.

printing money. In an attempt to control this situation, the government even declared inflation unlawful in 2007 forbidding any increase in the price of goods and services. Finally, in 2009, as the crisis reached its peak, the government removed the Zimbabwean dollar from circulation and the use of other currency such as the US dollar, the Euro, and the South African rand were made lawful.

Life during this period of hyperinflation was a daily struggle for ordinary people, many of whom were still being paid in Zimbabwean currency. A black market quickly developed but even so, basic foodstuff such as bread would be either unavailable or unaffordable. At present, Zimbabwe still has no national currency, using mostly US dollars and a combination of other foreign currencies.

ECONOMIC PROSPECTS

Zimbabwe's economy grew between 2009 and 2010 after the end of hyperinflation. However, its real GDP growth has fallen from 9 percent in 2010, 6.8 percent in 2011, and 4.4 percent in 2012. Zimbabwe's natural resources are a firm foundation for economic growth. However, growth hinges on a settlement of the country's political crisis. An urgent need is for the land issue to be resolved so that agricultural production can progress.

Forestry is a new economic resource that could become more profitable in the future. Large areas have been planted with softwoods that can be harvested for pulp. In the southwest of the country, there are new plantations of teak and mahogany.

A more controversial source of export income is the manufacture of ammunition. Factories based in the capital, Harare, produce high-explosive shells and other weapons for export, mostly to other African countries.

Men hard at work logging wood in a forest.

TOURISM

Tourists go on an elephant-back safari ride to explore the wilderness among Victoria Falls.

Tourism grew rapidly in Zimbabwe after independence. From less than 240,000 in 1980, the number of tourist arrivals more than doubled in a decade, to more than 550,000 in 1990. The figure exceeded 2 million in 1999, but violent invasions of commercial farms and clashes during elections have caused a dramatic drop of approximately 75 percent in tourist arrivals, as travelers choose to bypass Zimbabwe in favor of its more peaceful neighbors. This has led to lower hotel occupancy rates, the withdrawal of international airlines, and the loss of jobs in the tourism sector.

Tourism earns Zimbabwe around $400 million in foreign currency a year and accounts for approximately 5 percent of the gross domestic product. The Zimbabwe Tourism Authority is working to promote the country as a vacation destination by looking for new markets in Asia and the Middle East and organizing travel fairs. Efforts to revive tourism will have to address the root cause of the slump in the sector—the country's political problems and public violence. However, tourist arrivals have been on the rise, with 859,995 in the first half of 2013, up from 767,393 visitors during the same period in 2012.

EXTERNAL TRADE

Zimbabwe used to trade mainly with the United States, the United Kingdom, Germany, and African nations such as Botswana, Malawi, Mozambique, South Africa, and Zambia. However, since 2001, the United States, the United Kingdom and the European Union countries have imposed sanctions against Zimbabwe although today, these sanctions are being reviewed as ordinary Zimbabweans have suffered considerably under these sanctions.

Zimbabwe's major exports include tobacco, cotton, platinum, gold, ferroalloys, and textiles, while its major imports include machinery and transportation equipment, chemicals, fuels, and food products.

Zimbabwe is a member of regional economic organizations such as the Common Market for Eastern and Southern Africa, which aims to remove trade barriers in the region. The country is also one of 15 member states in the Southern African Development Community, which promotes development projects to raise the quality of life of people in the region and improve collaboration among member states.

UNEMPLOYMENT

According to NGOs, the unemployment rate stands at 85 percent at present. The number of people out of work remains high. Evidence of the problem can be seen in the city streets, where people with no formal occupation engage in knitting, basket weaving, and other craftwork. The government's failure to redistribute land on a scale big enough to satisfy the large number of poor people living in the rural areas has worsened unemployment. As people leave the countryside to find work in the urban areas, they have to invent ways to support themselves as there are not enough jobs.

INTERNET LINKS

www.mepip.gov.zw/

Official website of Zimbabwe's Ministry of Economic Planning and Investment Promotion providing information on investment sectors, ministry structure, and various departments.

www.indexmundi.com/zimbabwe/economy_profile.html

Official website of Index Mundi providing economic profile of Zimbabwe including overview, GDP statistics, unemployment rate, household income, and more.

www.africaneconomicoutlook.org/en/countries/southern-africa/ zimbabwe/

Website of the African Economic Outlook providing information on economic activity, data, and statistics.

ENVIRONMENT

Jacaranda trees blossom in full splendor in Bulawayo.

5

Z IMBABWE'S ENVIRONMENTAL ISSUES are closely connected to its economic issues. Poor industrial management and widespread poverty are big contributors to deforestation, soil erosion, pollution, and loss of wildlife. Other major environmental concerns that Zimbabwe faces include waste disposal and the depletion of natural resources.

WILDLIFE CONSERVATION

Wildlife conservation is one of Zimbabwe's biggest priorities. As in many countries with a rich wildlife and large human population, there is competition for living space in Zimbabwe between people—some 12 million of them—and plants and animals.

Fortunately, wildlife conservation efforts have achieved reasonable success in recognition of the economic value of nature. Zimbabwe's wildlife is a major attraction for tourists, who spend millions of dollars every year in the country's national parks and safari areas. As such, the government has provided substantial support for the upkeep of the country's national parks, which double up as conservation areas and ecotourism destinations. The best-known parks, such as Hwange, Mana Pools, Matusadona, and Victoria Falls, have proper facilities and trained guides to take visitors on walks or canoe rides through natural wildlife habitats while keeping precious species of flora and fauna safe from untrained or uncaring hands.

Zimbabwe's current major environmental problems include deforestation; soil, air and water pollution; and slash-and-burn agriculture resulting in soil erosion mainly caused by the land reform program.

There are several environmental movements in Zimbabwe that are dedicated to wildlife conservation. The oldest and largest, Wildlife and Environment Zimbabwe, with a global network and over 80 years of experience, leads the way in environmental research and national park development, among other things.

SAVING THE GIANTS

Zimbabwe is home to some mighty creatures. Some of them are native to Zimbabwe; a few live mainly in Zimbabwe; and others are found in other parts of Southern Africa as well. At least 14 species of mammals are endangered in Zimbabwe today, including the elephant, white and black rhinoceros, lion, cheetah, leopard, and more.

A majestic elephant stands near Lake Kariba. Many of these animals have been taken from the wild and shipped to other countries to be placed in zoos, which animal rights groups have protested.

ELEPHANTS Zimbabwe shares with neighboring Botswana the largest population of elephants in Africa. While that may impress visitors, large herds are not easy to support. Full-grown elephants need a lot of food and space. If they become too many for the area they inhabit, these gentle giants look for food elsewhere in the forest or savanna or on farmland, trampling crops and ground vegetation, and pushing down trees to eat the fruit and leaves.

Environmentalists have not been able to come to an agreement on the best way to approach this problem. While some advocate leaving the elephant population to a natural cycle of change over time, others support controlled culling—killing a fixed number in reserves every year. The latter option can also generate income from hunters who will pay large sums of money to experience the hunt. On moral grounds, however, culling remains unjustifiable.

In 2009, it was reported that the elephant population stood at approximately 100,000 although conservation groups have accused the authorities of inflating the figures to over 100,000 in order to continue to benefit from the lucrative ivory trade.

ALOE TREES

Aloes are hardy plants. They grow on rocky outcrops or cliffs in the drier areas of Zimbabwe. With their succulent leaves, they can survive with very little water. There are hundreds of species, some of which are shrubs and others trees as tall as 16 feet (5 m).

According to the World Conservation Union, Southern Africa has the largest concentration of succulent plants in the world, and a fifth of the traded species are threatened. Many aloe species, for example, have medicinal uses that render them vulnerable to commercial exploitation. Possibly around 10 percent of plants in Zimbabwe have been labeled threatened due in part to illegal trade.

There is a society in Zimbabwe that focuses its efforts on widening people's knowledge of aloes, cacti, and other succulent plants through research and walks and on working with similar organizations and the government authorities to conserve such plants. Conservation efforts include growing threatened indigenous species in parks. For example, the Ewanrigg Botanical Garden has a wide range of aloe plants.

The flowers of a flat-flowered aloe or *Aloe marlothii*, are a bright orange-red in color but varies from red to yellow, depending on the time of bloom.

Zimbabwe is party to the Action Plan for the Environmentally Sound Management of the Common Zambezi River System, or the Zambezi Action Plan, along with Botswana, Mozambique, Tanzania, and Zambia.

ENERGY AND THE ENVIRONMENT

Zimbabwe gets almost half of its energy from fossil fuels. Wood is the top fuel in rural areas, while thermal power plants burn coal. The burning of fossil fuels releases pollutants such as carbon monoxide and sulphur dioxide into the air.

Hydroelectric power is a cleaner source of energy. The power of the great Zambezi River has been harnessed by dams and power plants to generate electricity for industrial and residential activity in surrounding areas. However, damming rivers has negative effects on the natural environment.

THE ENDANGERED AND THE DANGEROUS

According to the World Conservation Union, Africa's black or hook-lipped, rhino is critically endangered, and the white, or square-lipped, rhino has been classified as near threatened. Zimbabwe is one of the last few places on earth where black and white rhinos survive.

The black rhino is poached for its horn which is used as a traditional medicine in Asia and carved for ceremonial dagger handles in the Middle East, despite a worldwide ban on trade in the horn. Trade in rhino horn fuels hunting that threatens the black rhino with extinction. The Zimbabwean authorities have resorted to drastic measures in attempts to ensure the future of some 430 black rhinos in the country. One alternative is to shoot rhino poachers; another is to move groups of rhinos to guarded locations. However, extinction remains a real possibility for the black rhino.

The "Save the Rhino" group reported that Zimbabwe's rhino population declined from about 830 in 2007 to 740 at the end of 2008 despite an excellent birth rate in monitored herds. It also reported that at least 90 rhino were poached in 2008; twice the toll of the previous year, and conservation groups had counted 18 killed so far in 2009.

There is also an increase in poaching of zebra for their hides which are used as upholstery in Europe. In contrast, hippos are common in Zimbabwe. They spend most of the day in swampy areas to keep their skin moist and forage on land in the evening. They can eat around 55 to 88 lbs (25—40 kg) of vegetation a day.

If prevented from returning to the safety of the water after feeding, or if people or other animals intrude upon their territory, hippos can get aggressive, especially if it is the mating season. With their huge bulk, big mouth and teeth, and surprising speed even on land, hippos can be dangerous. There have been reports of hippos attacking people and capsizing canoes.

Rivers and their valleys are the habitat of many species of plants and animals that depend on one another and on the flowing water for survival.

The Kariba Dam on the Zambezi between Zimbabwe and Zambia flooded forests in the late 1950s and stranded many animals on small islands. The then Rhodesian government launched Operation Noah to save the animals from drowning as the lake continued to rise. Rangers went out day after day in boats to the islands in Lake Kariba, caught thousands of animals such as antelopes and warthogs in nets, and then transported the animals back across the lake. Some of the animals, however, drowned before rescuers could reach them.

Almost all of Zimbabwe's coal-fired stations are in desperate need of improvement as a result of maintenance neglect over many years. Consequently, there are regular gaps in electricity production, leading to frequent blackouts, adding to the daily hardship of the people.

Another potential source of energy is sunlight. Solar power is already being used in Zimbabwe, but in very limited ways, such as to heat water in some households. Solar power accounts for a minute proportion of the country's energy. The development of this form of renewable energy is being hampered by the political challenges in the country today. Nevertheless, this clean form of energy has a lot of potential in sunny Zimbabwe. Increasing people's awareness of the usefulness of solar energy and manufacturing solar cells domestically to make them more affordable will help widen residential applications of solar power in Zimbabwe.

A thermal power station in Harare.

AIR POLLUTION

The quality of the air in Zimbabwe, especially in the larger cities, has deteriorated drastically since the 1990s, under the pressure of increasing industrial activity and road traffic. Besides the heavy traffic on Zimbabwean roads, many automobiles in the country are old and emit large amounts of pollutants, including poisonous lead particles and harmful gases such as carbon monoxide.

The big cities are also the most vulnerable to industrial sources of air pollution. In addition to being hubs of industrial activity, they are also population centers, and a lot of their heavy industry, such as chemical manufacturing and oil refining, is located near residential areas.

To reduce the harmful effects of industrial activity and road traffic on the quality of air, the government has enacted new laws that require drivers and manufacturers to equip their automobiles and plants with emission control devices. However, it will take some time to effectively enforce the laws and bring air pollution down to less dangerous levels.

WATER POLLUTION

Water pollution is an especially grievous problem in a country where drought is not an uncommon occurrence. As Zimbabwe urbanizes at a rapid rate, sewage treatment facilities have not developed fast enough to deal with the enormous amounts of domestic and industrial sewage generated by a growing population and manufacturing sector.

Pollutants spread diseases through water and pose a serious health threat. They render river water unsafe for drinking or agriculture. The authorities have considered making companies responsible for effluents that they release into natural waterways. Organizations will eventually be required by law to reduce water consumption to specified levels and to recycle used water. The government will also monitor the way plants discharge waste to ensure that they do not pollute rivers. Offenders will have to pay for the cost of cleaning up pollution that they cause.

The beautiful Chirinda Forest Reserve, where some of the tallest trees in Zimbabwe are found. The forest is a legacy left behind by the Dutch.

SOLID WASTE MANAGEMENT

To deal with litter in city streets, the Zimbabwean government has considered imposing penalties not only on consumers but on producers as well. The rationale is that if companies are made accountable for litter resulting from the consumption of their products, they will make efforts to reduce the amount of packaging they use.

The urban environment is also at risk due to infrequent garbage collection and poor treatment techniques. Waste left for days attracts disease-carrying pests, while incineration releases harmful gases and particles into the air. Waste management can be improved by hiring private companies to collect garbage and using new technologies to reduce and recycle waste.

DEFORESTATION

Deforestation and its effects on the country's flora and fauna are a grave environmental concern. Zimbabwe Electricity Supply Authority reported that it was only able to provide a third of the country's electricity demand. The poor production of electricity and regular blackouts have caused its people to cut down trees for domestic use such as cooking and heating. As a consequence, Zimbabwe lost more than 30 percent of its forest cover between 1990 and 2010.

The government launched a conservation campaign in 2012 with the title "Conserve Water and Stop Littering to Save Money and the Environment" in a bid to decrease pollution and lower the risk of water-borne diseases.

INTERNET LINKS

http://ecolocalizer.com/2008/07/30/zimbabwe-a-cry-for-the-environment/

Website of Eco Localizer providing information about the major environmental issues facing Zimbabwe today.

www.indexmundi.com/zimbabwe/environment_current_issues.html

Website of Index Mundi providing a breakdown of current issues in relation to Zimbabwe's environment.

www.zimwild.co.zw/

The official site of Wildlife & Environment Zimbabwe (WEZ) founded in 1927 providing information on the conservation and protection of Zimbabwe's environment.

ZIMBABWEANS

A modern family in Zimbabwe.

6

THE MAJORITY OF ZIMBABWEANS are Shona, while about 14 percent of the population are Ndebele. The Ndebele are a distinct people whose ancestors were warriors in the Zulu army. The strong ethnic difference between the Shona and the Ndebele has created difficulties for a nation state trying to forge a common identity.

During the first few years after independence in 1980, these differences erupted into violent conflict.

School children in Harare.

The adoption of the name "Zimbabwe" and the calling of its people as "Zimbabweans" symbolized the integration of all its different ethnic groups under a single national identity.

The Batonga are a minority group in Zimbabwe whose ethnic origins are uncertain. People of European descent make up the other minority group in the country.

THE SHONA

The ancestors of the Shona people crossed the Zambezi River into what is now Zimbabwe about 400 A.D. Today, Shona peoples make up about 82 percent of Zimbabwe's population and can also be found in Botswana, South Africa, Zambia, and Mozambique.

Traditionally, the Shona are farmers and cattle herders. Their rural lifestyle gradually evolved through centuries, but the arrival of the European settlers brought about drastic change. Although most of Zimbabwe's Shona population still live in the countryside, an increasing number now live in cities and towns as the rate of urbanization rises.

There are important subgroups within the Shona. The dominant subgroups are the Korekore in the north of Zimbabwe, and the Manyika and Ndau in the east. Almost half of the people in Southern Zimbabwe who speak the Shona language belong to the Karanga group. They are unique among the Shona, because they are more closely allied with the Ndebele despite their Shona ethnic ancestry.

The Shona make up the majority of the population, and it is hardly surprising that Shona-speaking people occupy many important political positions in Zimbabwe. The country's president, Robert Mugabe, is a Shona, and members of his party are predominantly Shona.

THE NDEBELE

While the Shona came to Zimbabwe looking for land to farm and graze their cattle, the Ndebele came in the mid-19th century as warriors. They eventually settled down as farmers but retained an army that was strong enough to

Although they form
only 14 percent of
the population, the
Ndebele people
have always played
a part in struggles
against foreign
domination.

deter the first European settlers from attempting an outright takeover. The very name of the main Ndebele city, Bulawayo, means place of slaughter. This is a reference to the violent struggles that took place among the Ndebele for the right to rule.

The Ndebele today are concentrated in the southwest of Zimbabwe around Bulawayo, where their ancestors first settled. No longer warriors as their ancestors, the Ndebele nevertheless have a strong sense of their unique history and separate identity.

They express this awareness in one of their proverbs: "*imbokodo kazicholelan*" (im-boh-KOH-doh kahz-ee-koh-LAY-lan), which means that grindstones don't grind for each other. Grindstones have been used since ancient times as a cutting tool to process grains and cereals. The Ndebele philosophy behind the proverb is that each grindstone has a different size, shape, and texture, and one does not put two stones together and expect them to fit perfectly. The implication is that each ethnic group has its own culture and way of life that cannot be easily integrated with that of another ethnic group.

Men who wear traditional clothing of the Ndebele tribe people sing and dance as part of a performance.

INTEGRATING INTO SOCIETY

After independence, the rivalry between the Ndebele and the Shona was developing into a civil war. The Shona central government sent troops into Ndebele areas to defeat the Ndebele-based opposition party. Terrible war crimes were committed by the government, and many innocent people were killed. In 1988 peace was established, and the Ndebele leader, Joshua Nkomo, who had fled the country, returned as vice-president.

Today, the peace seems to be a secure and permanent one, mainly because the source of conflict had more to do with worries about land resettlement than it did with ethnic differences. Zimbabwe's second university, located in the city of Bulawayo, is predominantly Ndebele, a sign that the country's most important minority group has become an integral part of the mainstream society.

Black and white students chat while waiting outside a classroom in a private Catholic school. Discrimination is still widespread, but encouraging interaction plays a role in helping the different races see eye-to-eye.

The Zimbabwean diasporas refers to the millions of black and white Zimbabweans who have immigrated to other countries mainly for political and economic reasons. The first diaspora was triggered by terrorism by the black liberation movement in the 1960s and 1970s. The second diaspora was made mostly by Zimbabweans feeling the dictatorship of Mugabe after independence in 1980 to the present day.

Many who have left have settled in countries including the United Kingdom, South Africa, Canada, United States, Botswana, and Australia. Those who leave to seek a better life come from the opposite ends of the socioeconomic spectrum — the affluent and educated, such as doctors and lawyers, who can find work abroad, as well as the poor and/or vulnerable who are forced to seek work and/or asylum abroad.

THE WHITE MINORITY

Out of Zimbabwe's population of more than 12 million, about 2 percent are not ethnically African. Of these, about 1 percent is Asian, or of mixed European and African descent, and less than 1 percent of European descent, most of whom trace their origins to Britain.

In the years of fighting leading up to independence, and immediately after the advent of black-majority rule, an average of 17,000 Europeans fled the country each year. Those who remained in the new state of Zimbabwe were given assurance that their farms and possessions would not be confiscated for at least 10 years, if at all.

The promise was initially kept. The large and prosperous farms, which covered vast tracts of the country's best land, remained under white ownership. These farms produced around 80 percent of the country's agricultural products, and the white owners maintained a high standard of living.

Before 1980 blacks were not able to vote, own the good land that had belonged to their ancestors, or have equal rights in crucial services such as education and health. Few whites had any understanding of the aspirations of the black majority. Many of those who did left the country and sought a life elsewhere.

Relations between whites and blacks reached their lowest point in the years between 1965 and 1980. Especially so after the launch of the land reform program in 1979. Once the white-minority government had broken ties with Britain in 2000, it felt free to pass laws that openly discriminated against blacks. During that time, the country came to resemble South Africa, with segregation being introduced into areas of public life.

THE WHITE POSITION TODAY

White farmers check the quality of their first batch of tobacco produce. In recent months, displaced farmers have called for talks with the government to help revive the agricultural sector.

In the 1990s, Mugabe used the issue of the concentration of wealth in white hands to gain reelection and secure political control. What followed was the seizure of white-owned farms in an atmosphere of violence and intimidation. Racial issues were resurrected as liberation war veterans stated a moral claim to the land of their ancestors.

Today, land ownership remains a divisive issue in Zimbabwe. At the same time, whites and blacks are uniting in opposition to ZANU-PF. The opposition party, MDC, is multiethnic in a way that no other political party has ever been in Zimbabwe. There were a handful of white Zimbabweans who took part in 2008. The hostility between whites (and MDC) and ZANU-PF continues into the next presidential polls.

Many whites who cannot accept the idea of equality are leaving the country, while the few who have chosen to stay have either moderated their views or kept them to themselves. Today, the white population amounts to only 30,000 people.

The legacy of European rule is still apparent in Zimbabwe. Old British cars can be seen on the roads. People drive on the left side of the road. The design of cities such as Bulawayo shows little African influence. Most apparent of all, perhaps, is the widespread use of English.

THE BATONGA

The Batonga are a minority ethnic group in Zimbabwe. Until the 1950s, they lived peacefully in the rural north of Zimbabwe, in a section of the Zambezi valley. The building of the Kariba Dam led to the flooding of their lands, and the group was split into two, one group on the Zimbabwe side, the other on the Zambia side of the river. Batonga families in Zimbabwe had to move farther south in the interior, away from the fertile valley and fresh water of the river.

The Batonga speak a dialect of Ndau, which shares a partial connection to the Shona language, and they have a rich tradition of music and storytelling.

Today, the Batonga are among the most poverty-stricken of all Zimbabweans. They used to make a living by selling their beadwork, but the high cost of materials has made the trade unprofitable. The government is making efforts to improve their standard of living, giving monetary grants to improve sanitation facilities and the water supply. For generations, the white-minority government ignored the Batonga, who had no access to education. This is changing as schools are built in Batonga communities.

A woman of Batonga descent smoking a water pipe in Zimbabwe.

INTERNET LINKS

www.bulawayo1872.com/history/shona.htm

Website providing information about the history of the Shona people of Zimbabwe.

www.bulawayo1872.com/history/ndebele.htm

Website providing information about the history of the Matebele Kingdom and the Ndebele tribe.

www.zimdiaspora.com/

Official website of *Zim Diaspora*, an online newspaper highlighting social and political injustice.

LIFESTYLE

A typically crowded market in Harare. Many people carry baskets on their heads to load daily neccessities and easily get through the hoards of people.

7

M OST ZIMBABWEANS LIVE in the countryside, but the cities continue to attract people in search of material quality of life. In the last century, the more productive land has been farmed by a minority of the people, while the majority struggled to make a living from infertile land.

This is still true to an extent, but life for the ethnic Africans, most of who live in the rural areas, has begun to change as schools and clinics are built in the countryside. Life remains hard, but the future looks more hopeful.

COUNTRYSIDE CONNECTION

Although the rate of urbanization continues to rise, many of the inhabitants maintain close ties with their families in the countryside. Every Friday, bus stations in urban areas are packed with people returning to their villages for the weekend. When they return to the city, they bring back fresh fruit and vegetables to sustain them until the following weekend.

LIFE IN THE COUNTRYSIDE

Life in the countryside is a blend of old and new. Farmers use chemical fertilizers to improve agricultural productivity, yet many cereal crops are still ground manually. Traditional attire has practically disappeared, but ancient rainmaking ceremonies still play an important role.

Life is a struggle for the majority of Zimbabweans who have to overcome daily challenges such as lack of water, food, and electricity.

A farmhand picks ears of corn in a field. The latest corn production amounted to more than 830,000 pounds, a significant difference from two million pounds in 2000.

A characteristic feature of life in the Zimbabwean countryside is people's dependence on walking as the main means of getting around every day. There is always a shop within walking distance, and villagers gather to buy things they need and at the same time chat and exchange news with the shop owner and with other customers. Owning a car is too expensive for most rural farmers. To travel long distances, such as between towns and villages, they hop on a bus.

A typical rural farmer often depends on the sale of his crops to earn money to support the family. However, unlike in the United States, in Zimbabwe small farmers use a large proportion of their crops to feed the family. They grow corn in their field and take the harvest on foot to the local mill for grinding. That corn serves as the staple food for the household. Firewood for cooking is collected on foot, and people have to walk farther as sources of wood become depleted. Fruit trees and vegetables are also cultivated in the countryside.

A noticeable feature of many village communities is the absence of young men, because they have left the countryside to find work in the cities. They return as often as they can, regarding the village as home, where their wives and children are. Many of the young men seek work on the big commercial farms or travel to towns to work in manufacturing plants. Some go to a different country, such as South Africa, for employment in the gold mines or in factories.

A WOMAN'S LIFE

Women grow more than half the world's food crops. In Africa, women account for as much as 60 to 80 percent of food production. As the men move to the towns and cities for work, more and more women are becoming heads of their households.

COMMUNAL LANDS

The "communal lands" were reserved for the ethnic Africans in Zimbabwe after the first European settlers arrived. The communal lands remain home to large numbers of Zimbabweans today. Before independence, life on the communal lands was extremely harsh. The quality of the soil was generally poor, making it impossible for farmers to increase their harvest without using fertilizers and machinery, which most farmers could not afford.

Since independence, the government has taken measures to help the families living in the communal lands. Pipes have been laid to improve water supply, and grants have been made available to the farmers so that they can buy chemical fertilizers. The increase in the production of corn had been astounding, and the communal lands produced much more corn than they did before 1980. In 1984, the growth rate of corn production was 11percent However, since the land reform program and severe drought corn production has decreased by 35 percent.

Besides the effects of drought and the conflict over the ownership of land, there are other serious problems. One of the most serious is soil erosion. The communal lands, made up of small family farms, contain more people than do commercial farmlands. Farmers in the communal lands also tend not to manage natural resources as well as large-scale farmers do. The constant need to collect firewood for cooking and timber for building homes and the large herds of cattle that eat the thin grass cover expose the topsoil to the elements of the weather—wind and water. A smaller cattle population might improve the situation, but farmers are reluctant to reduce their stock.

Soil erosion and drought have driven people from the communal lands. The violence and slow pace of land reform adds to the people's dissatisfaction.

Whether or not their husbands are in town, women in the villages have a daunting list of responsibilities, such as collecting firewood and water, cooking, looking after the children, and cleaning the home. They also maintain the vegetable gardens and work in the fields to sow the corn. Fertilizers increase corn yields, but more weeding needs to be done.

When their husbands are away working in the cities, the workload increases for the women in the villages. It then becomes their responsibility to look after the cattle and go to the market to sell the crops.

Women may have to bring their children with them wherever they go. If the child is very young, the mother may carry the child in a sling on her back. Women often carry their goods in a basket on the head. This not only frees their hands to hold their children's hands but also distributes the weight of the basket more evenly throughout the body and reduces the strain on individual muscles.

Despite the tremendous demands that they face every day in the fields and at home, women in the Zimbabwean countryside are not regarded as their husbands' equals. For example, according to tradition only men can inherit or rise to positions of power within a chieftaincy.

RIGHTS FOR WOMEN

They fought alongside men in the country's nationalist struggle, but Zimbabwean women today do not have equal legal status. Among the

Women collect water to be brought back to their village. The water is usually unsafe and unsanitary, which brings about threats to health, but it is the only source that the villagers have access to.

government's greatest challenges after gaining independence was to promote gender equality. The Legal Age of Majority Act was passed in the early 1980s, finally granting Zimbabwean women the right to vote and many other rights that were previously exclusive to male citizens.

Besides gaining greater access to education and employment, women have also become a force in the political and social spheres, as leaders, activists, or supporters. Opposition parties have won strong support from women voters drawn to the promise of gender equality.

In 1991 Zimbabwe acceded to the United Nations Convention on the Elimination of All Forms of Discrimination against Women. In 2008, the Maputo Protocol—which guarantees the right of women to take part in the political process, to enjoy social and political equality with men, to control their reproductive health, and to end female genital mutilation—was ratified. Women presently make up more than one-third of Zimbabwe's new Parliament. Yet women still face legal discrimination and lack land inheritance rights. It will take time for prejudice to break down and give way to true equality between women and men.

Women pounding maize for cornbread at a village in Zimbabwe.

A HARD LIFE

In the valleys of the Zimbabwe plateau, life is harsh. The sun glares, and temperatures reach 100°F (38°C) in summer. If there is no rain in winter, the region faces the possibility of drought. One of Zimbabwe's worst droughts occurred in 1992. However, in more recent years—in 2010, 2012, and 2013—drought has also severely affected many parts of the country causing thousands of families to suffer from a lack of a good harvest.

In the valleys far north, the tsetse fly makes it impossible to keep cattle. This means that farmers have to plows the land by hand. There are fewer schools and shops in the region than anywhere else in the country, and the absence of beer halls and markets testifies to a bleak social life for the inhabitants.

Serious droughts have caused fields of crops to dry out and wither.

A village in a poor Northern valley may consist of no more than a few mud-and-pole homes. Villages on the banks of a tributary of the Zambezi River have their own supply of fresh water. Otherwise, a well must be dug, or water must be carried from the nearest source. The woman of the household is up at five in the morning preparing breakfast before leaving for the day's work in the fields. In nearly every family, a father, son, or brother will likely be working outside the village out of economic necessity.

A successful harvest depends on rainfall after December. Without the rain, the cobs of corn and tufts of cotton will not appear. When the rain comes and the crops begin to grow, the fields are constantly raided by animals from the surrounding bushlands. Raids like these can easily destroy the best part of a harvest.

MARRIAGE

In Zimbabwe's rural communities, a young man will offer a large gift to the family of the woman he marries, and she will leave her village to live with him in his. The gift, often in the form of cattle, signifies the man's recognition of the woman's value and the link between their families.

When a woman marries, she adopts her husband's clan name. Clan members claim a common descent through the male line. Although a married woman will use the clan name of her husband, she can never actually become a member of the clan. If the marriage should prove unsuccessful, leading to a divorce, the woman returns to her father's home community and assumes his clan name again.

In the rural communities, it is possible for a man to marry more than one woman, although this is quite rare. When a man dies, his brother may inherit his wife, but she is free to reject a second marriage and go back to her father's village. In the case of divorce or the death of the husband, a woman may be disinherited by her husband's family and have to give up her home, money, and even children.

Many Zimbabwean women are speaking out against polygamy and against customary laws that leave women in a vulnerable position when their husbands die. In the towns and cities, traditional attitudes toward women and marriage are slowly changing. A lot more work needs to be done in the countryside, through education, to erode the assumption of male superiority.

The Ndebele hold initiation ceremonies to mark a person's passage from childhood to adulthood. The Shona mark a person's passage to adulthood by marriage and the birth of the first child. In that sense, marriage is considered natural and inevitable, and an unmarried man or woman can be regarded as an anomaly.

Children at a wedding party in Zimbabwe.

THE WEDDING GIFT The usual gift to the bride's family in rural marriages is cattle. For the Shona and the Ndebele, cattle are valuable for more than commercial reasons; cattle indicate a family's status and prestige. The larger a family's herd of cattle, the higher its status and the greater its prestige. The gift of cattle in marriage represents the man's commitment to the woman he marries.

BRIDE SERVICE In the poorer areas, a man may be unable to afford to offer cattle in exchange for his bride, or there may be no cattle because of a tsetse fly epidemic. Among the Korekore and the Tande, the husband often makes payment by leaving his village and setting up home in his wife's village, where he does bride service, or *kugarira* (kakh-ah-REE-rah). That means working in the fields of his father-in-law for a period of time, possibly 10 or even 15 years. Having fulfilled the bride service, the husband is allowed to return with his family to his own village. However, he may decide to stay if the family is well-settled. The wife's father may give her family land in the village for their use. The event is marked by various formalities, such as seeking permission from the ancestral spirits of the village for a stranger to join the community.

THE VILLAGE CHIEF

The chief of a rural community holds great social and political power, partly because he claims descent from the original owners of the land. They may be the first people ever to have lived there or the conquerors of the first inhabitants. There is a very strong feeling that the past is connected to the present through the chief, a living descendant of ancestors buried in the land. Significant sites, such as pools and hills, in a village are often named after ancestors, and stories relate how sites are connected with events in the lives of ancestors.

A native craftsman holds up straw baskets for sale in a fishing village.

The village chief's role has been changing for a long time. The early European settlers, who held tremendous political power, took away the age-old tradition of distributing land within the chief's territory. In the 1970s, during the struggle for independence, village chiefs who did not cooperate with the European government were replaced by new chiefs who were willing to support the government. Whole villages were resettled in the interest of security.

Contemporary life continues to erode the power of the village chief. The migration of people from the countryside to the cities weakens the chief's influence and power. Modern developments, such as business enterprises and women's cooperatives, do not fit under the traditional authority of the chief.

Traditionally, the village chief is spoken of as the father of his people, and his ancestors are their *sekuru* (sah-KOO-roo), or grandfathers.

URBAN LIFE

Over 38 percent of the country's population live in the towns and cities, but many more commute daily from the countryside to the urban centers for employment. The rate of urbanization is rising and between the periods 2010 to 2015, the rate of change is expected to be 3.4 percent. In the evening, many rural people head back to their villages. Harare, the capital city, is busier and livelier than anywhere else in the country. Its nightlife is enhanced by the high quality of the Zimbabwean music scene.

During the day, the busiest part of most towns is the market. People come in droves from the countryside to sell their vegetables and other agricultural products. The day's work begins well before dawn. As early as 4 A.M., stalls are stacked with fresh produce. Apart from food, the markets are centers for selling hand-dyed textiles and almost anything else that can be bought or sold.

Pedestrians cross a busy intersection in the city of Harare.

MBARE-THE URBAN HEART OF ZIMBABWE

First impressions of Harare can be deceiving. The tall buildings made of concrete and glass are typical of any international capital, and the city center has a remarkably sedate feel to it. Modern shopping centers, with names like Milton Park and Belgravia, lack any African identity, and suburban areas are still the preserve of middle-class European-descent families.

But a couple of miles away from the city center lies the densely populated area of Mbare. The urban pace of life in Mbare is most evident. Many of the inhabitants are poor, but there is little of the squalor associated with the poorer quarters of other cities. Mbare is home to the country's biggest market, the musika *(MOO-si-kah), and its busiest bus station.*

The musika is frenetically busy throughout the day, for merchants in the stalls do not sell things only to the individual consumer. Wholesale as well as bulk buying and selling goes on all day and porters wait with wheelbarrows to transport purchases.

One section of the musika is reserved exclusively for second-hand products. Enterprising stallholders there have an entirely new way of selling something old, for example, sandals made from old and worn-out car tires.

In 2005, a large area of Mbare was destroyed by the authorities under Operation Murambatsvina—a government campaign to clean up slums. Thousands of people lost their homes and means of livelihood.

The markets, which dominate life in all the urban centers in Zimbabwe, help to foster ties between the town and the countryside. But as modernization gathers pace, a very familiar pattern is becoming more evident in the larger towns—the emergence of an urban population born and brought up there. The younger generations in the cities have fewer and fewer ties with the rural past of their parents or grandparents.

As the trend continues, the lifestyle of urban Zimbabweans will begin to resemble more and more the features of life in any large city. Nevertheless, the distinguishing features of Zimbabweans are still to be found in the countryside.

THE FAMILY

Traditionally, children in Zimbabwe spend more time with their mothers than with their fathers, and the mother is responsible for the education and welfare of her children. One reason for this practice may be that men often have to leave their families to find employment away from home, in which case they may not see their children for months at a time.

The Western notion of a nuclear family, consisting of father, mother, and children, cannot be applied to traditional African society. A typical North American child has a clear sense of the difference between the immediate family structure and the extended family relationships that include uncles and aunts, cousins and grandparents.

A small Zimbabwean family consisting of a husband and wife with their young son.

The difference is far less obvious in traditional Shona and Ndebele society. Shona and Ndebele in rural areas are largely unfamiliar with the concept of a nuclear family structure. They relate to their relatives as members of one big family, or clan, and it is common for two or more generations to live together. Families are patrilineal, and when a man marries, he brings his wife to live with him in his settlement.

In the past, Zimbabwean men addressed their uncles as fathers and their aunts as mothers. Cousins were either sisters or brothers. However, industrialization and education have broken down extended family relationships. The term cousin is now increasingly used in the Western sense, and the terms uncle and aunt refer to a parent's brother and sister. Nuclear families are the norm in cities, although people still maintain strong links with their relatives.

Despite the process of modernization, the family structure is still a broader-based one than it is in the West. Illegitimacy and orphanhood are not perceived in the same way. An illegitimate or orphaned child would be more likely to find parents within the extended family.

EDUCATION

High school pupils share a desk in their classroom and study together.

Christian missionaries played a vital role in establishing schools for the ethnic Africans in Zimbabwe, but they were never able to overcome the institutionalized racism that benefitted the European population at the expense of the Africans. Today around one-third of the adult population has had no formal schooling.

Since 1980 the government has expanded elementary, intermediate, high-school, and college education in the country. Children are entitled to free elementary education, but child labor keeps some of them from completing elementary school. At the high-school level, more trained teachers are needed to meet the demands of the children.

Nevertheless, Zimbabwe has a higher literacy rate than many other African countries. More and more students are finishing high school and qualifying for admission to a university. Unfortunately, the University of Zimbabwe and the University of Science and Technology in Bulawayo are unable to offer places to all who are qualified.

Sadly, the problems in Zimbabwe today have adversely affected the state of education as a result of a lack of funding, shortage of teachers, materials and low salary. Teachers are some of the lowest paid professionals in the country and many are leaving the profession which leads to a decline in the quality of teaching. Teachers have gone on strike in recent years to protest against their working conditions. All these difficulties caused the school year in 2008 to be cancelled. In 2009, attendance rates in schools, particularly in rural schools, fell drastically from approximately 80 percent to 20 percent. Although education is free, there are fees for school enrollment which have been increasing steadily. Consequently, more and more children are not being educated as their families simply cannot afford the fees.

HEALTH

One of the biggest public health challenges faced by Zimbabwe today is the fight against AIDS. It is thought that as many as 1.2 million people in Zimbabwe, or 1 in 10 adults, are HIV-positive. AIDS is now the leading cause of death among children under age 5, many of whom are born to HIV-positive mothers. Prominent Zimbabweans in government, entertainment, and sports have died from AIDS.

The government finds it difficult to control the spread of AIDS. People are not educated about the disease and do not think that they can get it. In Zimbabwe AIDS is usually spread through unsafe sex. Hospitals do not have enough beds to treat AIDS patients, and most of them receive inadequate care.

Apart from AIDS, health professionals also have to deal with cholera outbreaks. Other more prevalent diseases afflicting the people of Zimbabwe include tuberculosis and malaria.

INTERNET LINKS

www.livingzimbabwe.com

Website providing unique insight into life in Zimbabwe through the views and opinions of ordinary people covering a wide range of topics from culture, politics, business, and more.

www.mhet.ac.zw/

Official website of the Ministry of Higher and Tertiary Education of Zimbabwe whose aim is to provide an effective system for the production of high level manpower through the provision and education.

www.mohcw.gov.zw/

Official website of Zimbabwe's Ministry of Health and Child Welfare which provides details of internal departments and agencies, services and minister profiles.

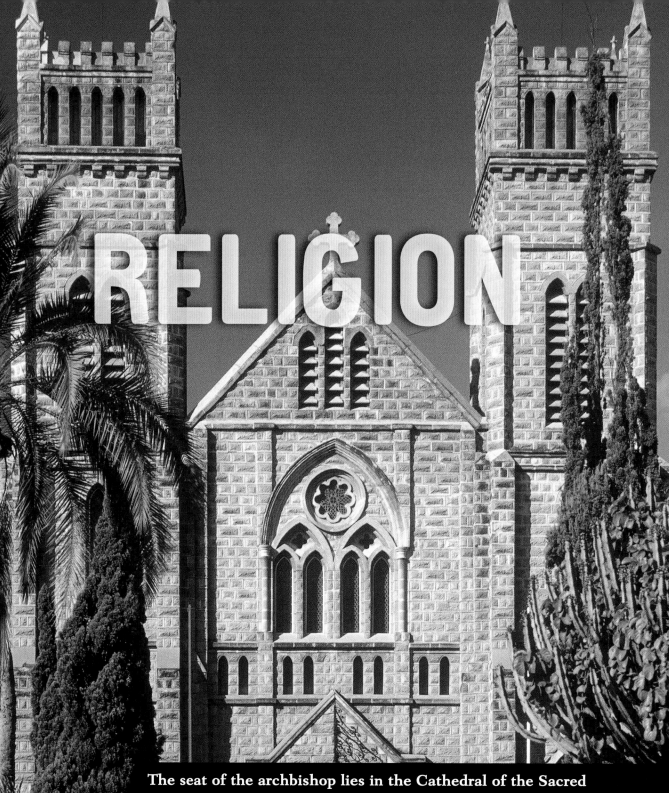

RELIGION

The seat of the archbishop lies in the Cathedral of the Sacred Heart in Harare.

8

M OST ZIMBABWEANS continue to practice their indigenous religions. They believe that the spirits of their ancestors have an important effect on the present. They seek the advice of ancestral spirits in all areas of life. During the nationalist struggle for independence, it was considered very important to have the support of an ancestral spirit medium who spoke in favor of the rebellion.

Fifty percent of people practice a mixture of Christianity and indigenous beliefs. 25 percent are Christian, 24 percent practice indigenous beliefs and 1 percent is Muslim.

The thatched Cyrene Mission in Bulawayo was established in 1939 by Canon Edward Paterson, an artist and missionary, who served the mission until his retirement in 1953,

A traditional village healer carrying out a healing ritual on a villager.

Christianity (the Apostolic, Pentecostal, Protestant, Roman Catholic and others) was introduced to the country by European missionaries who set up churches and schools for the ethnic Africans. Many of Zimbabwe's political leaders and prominent citizens were brought up as Christians and educated in Christian mission schools.

In recent years, however, the spread of mainstream Christianity in Zimbabwe has declined. What has increased, on the other hand, is the number of independent African churches that combine Christian and traditional indigenous beliefs and practices. Roughly half the Zimbabwean population belong to these syncretic religious groups.

TRADITIONAL RELIGION

Most world religions have some traits in common: a central store of set beliefs and rituals, sacred books, a history of its spread, and a name: Christianity, Islam, Buddhism, Hinduism, and so on. African religious beliefs and practices tend not to have such characteristics and, in the absence of a formal name, are referred to as traditional. The word traditional also points to the fact that such beliefs and practices were in existence long before Christianity or Islam made its impact in Africa.

The main animist cult in Zimbabwe worships a creator god called Mwari (m-WAHR-ee), who is believed to abide in the sky. In times of natural disaster, war, or other social disturbance, contact with Mwari is made through a spirit medium.

Obligations to care for family members are not taken lightly and do not come to an end at the time of death. After death, people are transformed into midzimu *(mid-ZEE-moo), or ancestors. As* midzimu, *they continue their roles as protective parents, but they wield more power than they ever did when alive. Ancestors perceive what is happening among their living descendants and intervene when they feel it is necessary. They do not act irresponsibly. They might signal to warn of approaching danger or request that a child be named in their memory. One method of showing that they wish to be heard is by causing illness.*

POWER OF THE SPIRITS

Zimbabweans who practice their indigenous religions believe in powerful ancestral spirits that influence life in ways people cannot control or sometimes even understand. People worship the spirits to appease them and win their favor.

Unlike Mwari, the Supreme Being, ancestral spirits were once human beings and are thus believed to be more accessible and understandable to the living. The spirits of ancestors are thought to live in a land located under the ground, where they are able to keep watch over the living.

If the spirits are unhappy about something, they send signs of their displeasure. When sickness or a natural calamity occurs, animists may interpret it as a sign that they have offended the spirits. They then go to a shrine, which may be a cave or a tree, to ask the spirits to put things back to normal.

People communicate with ancestral spirits in various ways. They may offer prayers or sacrifices. The most dramatic way is through ritual specialists. They include rainmakers or mediums who can be contacted in order to find

A medicine man's market stall.

the source and the solution of a particular problem. In the case of drought, for example, a Shona rainmaking spirit medium may be contacted to negotiate with the particular spirit that is causing the lack of rain and keeping the crops from growing.

The spirit of a village chief is of special importance. When he dies, he becomes a *mhondoro* (meh-HOHN-doh-roh), which is responsible for the continued fertility of the land in which he was once the guardian. If the will of the *mhondoro* is obeyed, rain will come on time and the crops will grow. If his advice is ignored or a crime is committed, then the rain may be withheld. All the men who work on the land of the *mhondoro* make annual offerings of grain at the first harvest.

SPIRIT MEDIUMS

According to traditional African religion, when an ancestor wishes to communicate with its descendants, a woman or man is possessed by the spirit, who speaks through the mouth of the chosen person. The possessed person then becomes a spirit medium.

Mediums are often ordinary people who appear to be ill. If the illness is not easily cured, it is suspected that a spirit has possessed the person. In other parts of Africa, the act of possession is usually spontaneous, but among the Shona, it takes place at organized rituals. The purpose of the ritual is to confirm that a possession has actually taken place and to establish the spirit's identity.

Such rituals are carefully prepared and often dramatically performed. Beer will be brewed and a team of drummers engaged for the occasion. Relatives and friends will travel from other villages to attend the ritual, which is usually held on a weekend.

During the ceremony, experienced mediums beat drums and dance to call up the spirit. The dancers dress in black and white and carry ritual axes and spears. If the sick person is possessed, he or she will join in the dancing. The person is later questioned and, as the spirit speaks through him or her, the questioners try to establish its identity—whether it is an ordinary spirit, the spirit of an ancestor, or the spirit of a chief.

An important medium, one possessed by the spirit of a chief, is expected to look and behave in a way that suggests the chief himself has returned to life. Unlike almost everyone in Zimbabwe today, the spirit medium does not wear Western-style clothes. His main attire consists of two pieces of cloth, one wound around the waist and reaching to the ankles, the other slung across the shoulder. The medium wears sandals and sometimes a fur hat. Carrying a staff and ritual ax, he resembles a Shona chief.

Anyone dealing with the medium is expected to remove shoes and headgear and is forbidden to carry a rifle. This is a direct throwback to the days when a chief protected himself by forbidding people to carry weapons in his presence.

Once a medium's reputation is established, he or she can practice professionally. Many mediums dedicate their lives to this calling. They receive payment for curing illnesses or bringing rain, but are expected to use most of the money to maintain their shrine. If they grow rich from their practice, they may be accused of fraud, and their reputation and future as a medium suffers.

Villagers performing an ancestral dance.

THE SPIRIT OF NEHANDA

Nehanda was a chief, and so her spirit became a mhondoro. In the first rebellion of 1896 against the European settlers, a medium of Nehanda played a major role in leading the uprising. She was eventually captured and hanged, but her defiance became legendary. Tales and songs circulated about her refusal to accept conversion to Christianity and the prophetic words she declared from the scaffold that her bones will rise to defeat the Europeans.

When the second uprising began in 1972, the rebels found that many spirit mediums were once again on their side. Mhondoro spirits continued their responsibility to protect the land, and the nationalist demands for returning land from the European minority to the African majority seemed the best way to do this.

After the death of Nehanda's first medium, the mhondoro resided with another medium, which was committed to helping the rebels. The government forces were well aware of the danger posed by the spirit mediums and distributed tape recordings and posters of mediums who were against the African nationalists.

Afraid that the government forces might capture and punish the medium of Nehanda, the nationalists persuaded her to cross the Zambezi River and hide in Mozambique. She stayed there until her death in 1973, when she was given a funeral fit for a chief. She was carried to her grave in a white cloth and buried on a wooden platform in the ground, surrounded by a hut that had been built and thatched in a day.

In that respect, mediums are different from traditional healers, for whom it is not taboo to become wealthy through their profession. Traditional healers also do not come in contact with ancestral spirits and are free to conduct their business according to personal preferences. The life of a medium, however, is bound by tradition and convention.

WITCHES

Animists in Zimbabwe believe in witches, or *muroyi* (merh-ROI-ee), who ride about not on broomsticks but on the backs of hyenas. Witches are believed to be responsible for unpleasant deeds such as robbing graves and killing people and turning them into animals. Less dramatically, their presence is felt when a traditional healer or a spirit medium attributes an illness to a spell cast by a witch.

An unfortunate person may become a witch through possession. If this happens, it is passed down from generation to generation, not only from mother to daughter but also from father to son. It is also believed that a witch can be found within one's family.

Witches are so feared that the only effective way to deal with them is to kill them. Beliefs like these can lead to terrible tragedies, especially as possession of a family member is very common. Even today, it is not uncommon to read accounts of deaths occurring in this manner.

The fear of witches is also reflected in rites that take place at some funerals. At the bottom of the grave, a shelf is hollowed out where the body is placed before being covered with a mat and poles. The grave is then filled with stones and earth, and large rocks are piled on the site, forming a large mound.

A witch doctor dressed in an elaborate fashion.

These rites are carried out in order to make it more difficult for a witch to reach the body. The surrounding area is also carefully swept, so that if a witch attempts to approach the grave, footprints will be left.

WITCHCRAFT SUPPRESSION ACT   Witchcraft is recognized by Zimbabwean law, although there are problems in defining exactly what constitutes witchcraft. Established at the end of the 19th century and amended in 1989, the Witchcraft Suppression Act declares it illegal to practice witchcraft, or sorcery, or to accuse someone of practicing witchcraft. Offenders may be punished with imprisonment.

In 1997 the Zimbabwe National Traditional Healers Association (ZiNaTHA) proposed a second amendment to the act, to restrict the prohibition of witchcraft to only those acts aimed at causing disease or injury to another person or to an animal. Churches and human rights organizations have generally opposed the proposal. An amendment to the Witchcraft Suppression Act in 2006 criminalized witchcraft practices only if intended to cause harm. Under this new framework, spoken words alone would no longer be considered a witchcraft practice or proof of illegal activity.

CHRISTIANITY

Christianity came to Zimbabwe through missionaries in the latter half of the 19th century. Today Christianity has an established role in Zimbabwe as the predominant belief system outside of traditional African religion.

About one quarter of Zimbabwe's population are members of typical Christian churches. Of that number, more than one-third are members

The interior of Mvurwi Church, a catholic church in the Mashonaland Central province.

of independent churches. The Roman Catholic and Anglican churches have the largest number of followers. The Methodist and Congregational churches are the two largest Protestant groups. The growth of Christianity in the country has slowed considerably since independence.

The established churches have a mixed relationship with traditional African religion. Some churches have been more receptive than others to the local people's traditional beliefs and customs.

For example, it is not uncommon for the members of certain churches to attend a Sunday morning service after having spent the night at a possession ceremony. Or they might wear a string of black ancestral beads as well as a cross around the neck. In the countryside especially, people would not have a problem attending Christian church services on a regular basis while continuing to participate in possession ceremonies and make offerings to the local *mhondoro*.

Evangelical churches, on the other hand, are actively opposed to the traditional religions of Zimbabwe. They perceive animist beliefs and practices as ungodly. The drinking of beer, an established part of possession ceremonies, is banned during the services of Evangelical churches in the country. The members of those churches are strictly forbidden from participating in other ancestral rituals as well.

MISSIONARIES

Christian missionaries first arrived in Zimbabwe, then Rhodesia, with Cecil Rhodes at the end of the 19th century. Due to their involvement in politics—for example, it was a missionary who negotiated a treaty for Rhodes tricking the

Christians come to church to partake in and observe Sunday service.

A Sister of the Victoria District Bondolfi Mission educating the village children on the use of drums.

Ndebele leader Lobengula into signing away his people's rights—missionaries were attacked and murdered in the uprising of 1896.

They continued to come after the uprising was put down, and by 1910 there were more African than European Christians in Rhodesia.

Missionaries played a crucial role in educating the Africans. Wherever a church was built, a school followed. Roman Catholic, Anglican, and Methodist missionaries were among those who set up churches and schools in Zimbabwe. Many also established clinics and hospitals, which were often the only places where the ethnic Africans could have access to Western medicine. The missionaries brought many benefits, but their beliefs were often at odds with traditional beliefs.

Missionaries faced a dilemma during the 1970s when the nationalists fought the government. Many supported the nationalists, but many died in the war. While the government blamed the nationalists for the deaths of the missionaries, the nationalists blamed the government.

Today Christian missions continue to flourish in Zimbabwe. Some mission schools are better funded than government schools and provide better education. Many of Zimbabwe's leading citizens, including Robert Mugabe, were educated in mission schools.

THE VAPOSTORI

The Apostolic Church strongly opposes ancestral worship. Members of the Apostolic Church, known in Zimbabwe as the Vapostori, spend time exorcising ancestral spirits, or what they consider to be witches.

The Vapostori believe that prayer is the only remedy for disease and illness of both the body and the spirit. They not only oppose traditional medicine but also reject orthodox Western medical practices. This has resulted in distressing cases where children die unnecessarily because their parents refuse to consider using available drugs. The Vapostori, who mainly reside in Manicaland, have high levels of infant and maternal mortality rates partly because they shun the use of medicine, believing that prayer is more powerful.

The Vapostori follow strict rules and isolate themselves from society, avoiding state education and law. This has led to a degree of conflict with the government, which wants to see them become more integrated with the rest of society.

INTERNET LINKS

http://relzim.org/

Website of Religion in Zimbabwe providing an overview of all the major religious faiths practiced in Zimbabwe today. The site includes news, a forum, social ministry, and education.

www.newzimbabwe.com/pages/witchcraft.14063.html

Online article from website of newzimbabwe.com on law and witchcraft in Zimbabwe.

www.nationsencyclopedia.com/Africa/Zimbabwe-RELIGIONS.html

Website of Nations Encyclopedia providing statistics on the various key religions of Zimbabwe.

LANGUAGE

A teenage girl reading from a storybook. Zimbabwe boasts a relatively high literacy rate, where 8 out of 10 people over 15 years of age can read and write.

9

THE THREE OFFICIAL LANGUAGES in Zimbabwe are Shona, Ndebele and English. Ndebele and Shona are the official languages of instruction.

Shona is the mother tongue of nearly 7 out of 10 Zimbabweans, while Ndebele—also known as Sindebele—is a minority language spoken by about 15 percent of the population. While Shona is spoken across the whole country, Ndebele speakers are concentrated around Bulawayo and the southwest of the country.

English is spoken everywhere. Even in remote rural areas, there is usually someone who can communicate in English. In the larger urban areas, English is widely spoken and is the language of business and government. The middle classes use English partly as a status symbol.

BANTU

There are more than 60 million people who speak Bantu as their native language. Both Shona and Ndebele are classified as Bantu languages. Other minor Bantu languages spoken in Zimbabwe are Tonga and Venda. Bantu is the general term for a wide family of languages spoken throughout the southern half of Africa that are believed to have a common origin. The original Bantu language was likely spoken in western Africa, from where it spread south and east. Over thousands of years, Bantu evolved into a large number of languages that are spoken in many areas of Africa. The most widespread Bantu language today is Swahili, spoken in many countries in eastern Africa.

SHONA

Before the European missionaries arrived toward the end of the 19th century, the Shona language did not exist in the form in which it exists

There are a total of 20 individual languages spoken in Zimbabwe today including Shona, Ndebele, English, Kalanga, Manyika, and Ndau.

today. Instead, different ethnic groups in Rhodesia spoke different dialects, which made the European missionaries' task of teaching the gospel ever more difficult. The missionaries made a systematic study of the different dialects spoken. The dialects were later brought together and unified under the common label Shona.

The Shona language includes the major dialects Karanga, Korekore, and Zezuru, and their subdialects. Zezuru is spoken in the capital and the surrounding district and is considered very prestigious to use.

People and dialects mix freely in Harare, and an urban form of Shona has evolved. Known as Town Shona or Chishona, it is characterized by a mixture of English and Shona words. Chishona abandons many of the more formal aspects of regular Shona. For example, in Shona, various pronoun forms are used to denote respect when addressing a person who is perceived as a superior. But in Chishona, dialogue takes place without these pronoun forms.

Local men share a friendly chat outside a shop.

The very first novel—*Feso*—in the Shona language was published in 1957 and written by Zimbabwean poet and author Dr. Solomon Mutswairo. This political novel features traditional African literary techniques such as song and storytelling. It was banned in 1960s by the government.

NDEBELE

When the Ndebele people moved from Zulu lands north into Zimbabwe during the first half of the 19th century, they spoke a Zulu dialect. In the course of time, other groups with their own dialects merged with the Ndebele, and the Ndebele language developed its own characteristics.

Nevertheless, a Ndebele in Zimbabwe and a Zulu would have little trouble understanding each other. The Ndebele spoken in Zimbabwe is more closely related to Zulu than to the versions of Ndebele spoken in South Africa. The version of Ndebele spoken in Zimbabwe is known as the Northern Ndebele language while the version spoken in South Africa is called the Southern Ndebele language. These two versions, however, have not originated from the same language although they belong to the Bantu group of languages. Ndebele is also spoken in Botswana.

LANGUAGE AND POLITICS

Nearly a century of European minority rule has had a permanent effect in Zimbabwe. English remains firmly established as an official language. In neighboring Mozambique, the language of the Portuguese colonists who once ruled the country still has a presence but not to the same extent that English does in Zimbabwe.

The reason for this is not that Zimbabwe has a patriotic attachment to the language of its colonial rulers. It simply reflects the fact that English is an important international language. English facilitates international trade and commerce and serves as a common language for the Shona and Ndebele peoples.

After independence, however, there was a need or desire among the people to mark their freedom in many areas of life, including language. The country's name, Rhodesia, evoked memories of the colonial era and even suggested a lack of history before the arrival of Rhodes and his followers. The name Zimbabwe, on the other hand, went back centuries to the time of Great Zimbabwe, and confidently asserted the people's sense of cultural identity.

Similarly, the capital, called Salisbury by the Europeans, was renamed Harare, after a tribal chief who had once ruled the area. Some important roads and streets in Harare were also given new names to remove their English character and glorify those who had played a significant role in the nationalist struggle in the 1970s.

The names of many towns have also been changed. Fort Victoria is one of the oldest established towns in the country, having served as a resting post for European travelers and explorers throughout the second half of the 19th century. It was named after the queen of England at that time, as was

Children lift cardboard signs during a lesson to learn the English names of various animals.

the nearby Victoria Falls. While the town is now officially called Masvingo, Victoria Falls has not been renamed.

Zimbabwe's biggest and most impressive wildlife park, Hwange National Park, was originally called Wankie National Park, a legacy of the colonial era. Hwange was the name of a local chief.

Other name changes corrected colonial mispronunciations. The town of Gwelo, for example, is now Gweru, while Matobo is now Matopos.

NONVERBAL COMMUNICATION

Some of the most appealing forms of nonverbal communication in Zimbabwe deal with etiquette—conventional rules of behavior that govern certain areas of social life.

When accepting a gift, both hands may be held out. This does not suggest that more is expected. Rather, it is an expression of gratitude. Sometimes the person receiving the gift will clap, and then hold out both hands, palms up, with fingers slightly crossed to make a kind of shallow spoon. Sometimes only one hand is held out, with the other held across its wrist, reflecting an old warrior's show of friendship.

Handshakes differ among men and women. Men slap their hands loudly, with the flat of one hand in line with the palm of the other hand. Women greet by slapping each other's palms gently. To greet a very important person, men will sit on the ground, clap their hands twice or three times, and wait silently for about 10 seconds, before clapping their hands again.

Formality governs certain occasions, such as a stranger visiting a village where a meeting, or *indaba* (IN-da-bah), is taking place. The newcomer approaches the circle of seated men, squats on its perimeter, and claps his hands gently two or three times.

Nobody says anything until the most senior man in the indaba stops talking and allows the others to continue. The visitor waits for a natural break in the conversation, and then claps again. If he is welcome, the senior man claps back as an invitation to join the group. Usually, a visitor to a village is greeted by a line of men clapping gently, and women making shrill sounds.

CHILAPALAPA

Chilapalapa (chill-ah-PAHL-ah-pah) is an English hybrid dialect influenced by the Ndebele and Shona languages. It developed during the colonial era to facilitate communication between the European farm owners and their African employees. Most of the communication took the form of orders and instructions. This is reflected in the grammar of the language, as the verbs only take the imperative form. For example, there is no verb "to leave," only the imperative form "Leave!" Some examples of Chilapalapa *words are* amanzi *(water),* ukudla *(food),* uchago *(milk).* Chilapalapa *is still used in some European households employing African workers, but it is dying out.*

A chicken, a pumpkin, or a handful of eggs may be given as a departing gift. As an expression of affection, the host and neighbors will escort visitors out of the village and accompany them for a mile or so.

Shona children are taught by their mothers to greet their fathers by clapping their hands and shouting "Kwaziwai baba" (Greetings to you, father). They are also taught a series of greetings for their grandfathers, grandmothers, and male and female neighbors.

INTERNET LINKS

www.shonalanguage.info/

Website with introduction to the language, which is spoken in Zimbabwe, as well as links to other Shona-related sites.

www.omniglot.com/writing/ndebele.php

Website of Omniglot providing an overview and information on the pronunciation of the Ndebele language including sample texts and useful links.

www.ethnologue.com/show_country.asp?name=ZW

Website of Ethnologue providing detailed information on the different languages spoken in Zimbabwe today.

ARTS

The National Gallery of Zimbabwe in Bulawayo, a major art institute, exhibits contemporary art in the form of paintings and sculptures, to name a few.

10

WHATEVER ZIMBABWE LACKS in material wealth, it is amply compensated for by a rich artistic tradition. This covers a wide range of art forms, including music, literature, sculpture, and dance.

Zimbabwean art has seen a renaissance since 1980, as political independence has given artists in diverse fields the freedom to express themselves and make themselves known to the country and the world. A *manyawi* (mahn-YAH-wi), the spirit of expression and excitement, is in the air.

A traditional African hut with decorative painting and thatched roof in the Matobo National Park of Zimbabwe.

Dance permeates
all aspects of
Zimbabwean life,
from religious
rituals to
political rallies.

MUSIC

Zimbabwe's most accomplished and independent art form is music. Zimbabwean music has developed its own identity and style. Some Zimbabwean musicians and bands have become successful enough to tour abroad and entertain people in other nations with their distinctive sounds.

Zimbabwean music defies categorization. It is a blend of African and other cultural influences, fusing rock, jazz, soul, and reggae with the sounds of traditional African instruments. The result, the music of Zimbabwe, has been dubbed Jit Jive or the Harare beat. Bands that have popularized this type of dance music include the Bhundu Boys.

What distinguishes Zimbabwean music is the use of three particular instruments: drums, a thumb piano, and a marimba. These traditional African instruments were much neglected during the colonial era. Western music followed different rules of harmony from those that governed the music of Africa, and the European colonialists sometimes regarded African music with indifference. Independence returned Zimbabwe's traditional musical instruments to the forefront.

A group of Marimba players.

THOMAS MAPFUMO AND THE BLACKS UNLIMITED

Thomas Mapfumo and his band have achieved international recognition, but for a long time they struggled to be heard. Before independence, Mapfumo made no secret of his opposition to European rule. His political songs were not popular with the government, and he suffered arrest and imprisonment. Today, Thomas Mapfumo and the Blacks Unlimited produce some of the finest Zimbabwean music, including pieces such as Gwindingwi Rine Shumba and Hokoyo, which are available in North America and Europe. Thomas Mapfumo is respected as a revolutionary figure in Zimbabwe who uses his music to fight for political change. He now lives in exile in the United States.

DRUMS Drums of different sizes provide a range of tones and pitches for Zimbabwean rhythms. Carved from a solid block of wood, with a membrane made from antelope or goat hide, the drums are often decorated with colorful designs.

The tone of a drum is affected by the tightness of the membrane. To loosen the membrane, one might heat it over a fire, whereas laying wax or heavy pieces of leather on the membrane stretches and tightens it.

There are three types of drum: *nhumba* (NOOM-bah), *dandi* (DAN-dee), and *mhito* (MEE-toh).

THE MBIRA The mbira (merh-BIRAH), a thumb piano, is a wooden soundboard with metal strips of varying lengths that are plucked to produce a melody. It is often used during religious rituals by mediums to communicate with ancestral spirits. In bands, the mbira is accompanied by singing, drums, and the *hosho* (HOH-shoh), a gourd partially filled with dried seeds that rattle against the inside of the gourd when the hosho is shaken. Mbiras are believed to be ancient instruments, dating back to the 12th century.

THE MARIMBA The marimba is a xylophone with wooden strips of varying lengths, each producing a different tone when struck with a rubber mallet. There are marimbas with different ranges, such as soprano or tenor. The type of wood used affects the sound quality.

The pitch of each wooden strip is adjusted by varying the thickness of the strip along its length—making a strip thinner in the middle lowers its pitch, and making it thinner at the ends raises its pitch. Hollow gourds or dried shells may be placed under the strips to increase the volume.

Schools in Zimbabwe often form marimba bands that perform in community halls and at school events. Traditionally, the marimba was played only by men, but today women also play it.

DANCE

In both Western and African culture, dance can function as recreation, entertainment, or a means of courting. Dancing is also appreciated by both cultures as an art form in its own right.

A significant feature of dance in Zimbabwe is its use as a means of expressing spirituality. Traditional African dance reflects a belief in the spirit of the earth as the provider of fertility. African dance usually has a downward orientation—toward the earth—with the feet planted on the ground in firm

A dance troupe wearing ankle bells, which draw attention to their footwork, entertains a large group of spectators.

steps and the knees flexed. Rainmaking ceremonies also involve dancing, and some of the evangelical churches in Zimbabwe incorporate dance into their worship. Some of Zimbabwe's most well-known dances include the religious Dinhe dance, the Jerusarema dance, which represents the Shona culture, and the Muchongoyo dance, which represents the Ndebele culture.

THE SHONA PROTEST SONG

The Shona protest song is based on a traditional genre. Protest songs are used to express a variety of emotions, such as sorrow over death or joy of victory in battle. Protest songs are sung by a group; the lead guitarist sings the main storyline, while the other band members sing the chorus. The audience joins in the singing by urging the band to *dzepfunde* (zep-FAHNDE), or go on.

In the years leading up to Zimbabwe's independence, the emergence of protest songs reflected a growing political consciousness among the people. Zimbabwean music of that time reflected revolutionary themes and became a tool to motivate people in the struggle for independence.

"God Bless Africa," a song composed in South Africa in 1897 by Enoch Sontonga and later translated into the languages of the Shona and Ndebele, became the song of resistance to European rule in Zimbabwe and was sung as a mark of triumph on the day of independence. It has since become the national anthem of South Africa.

SCULPTURE

Zimbabwe's most famous sculptors include Joseph Ndandarika, Sylvester Mubayi, Henry Munyaradzi, and Nicholas Mukomberanwa. Also making an impact in Zimbabwe is the Tengenenge (ten-gen-ENG-ay) school of sculpture. The name comes from a community that specializes in carving serpentine, a

Together We Shall Die, a sculpture by Joseph Ndandarika, known as the greatest sculptor of his generation, is a reference to the country's war of independence.

dull green rock with markings that resemble those of a serpent's skin. The community was founded in the 1960s by Tom Blomefield, who took up sculpting when his tobacco farm ran into financial difficulties.

A few Zimbabwean sculptors—including Moses Mosaya—have made it on the international scene, but for many aspiring sculptors the cost of transporting a piece of work to Europe or North America is a big hindrance.

Stone-carved sculptures are made by the locals in Zimbabwe.

THE GROWTH OF LITERATURE

Zimbabwe had a rich literary tradition before the printed word reached Africa. Early Zimbabwean poems, songs, and stories were passed down orally through memory from one generation to the next for centuries. Traditionally, the *sarungano* (sahr-oon-GAH-noh), or storyteller, was an elder who had lived a long and meaningful life.

The first foreigners to take an interest in early Zimbabwean literature were Christian missionaries. They transcribed the indigenous languages using the Roman alphabet and translated parts of the Bible for the local people. Modern Zimbabwean writers criticize the early missionaries for rejecting many religious beliefs that formed a part of the country's early literary tradition.

Before 1980 African writers in Rhodesia faced a major obstacle in the Rhodesian Literature Bureau. Any material proposed for publication had to be approved by the bureau. This was the minority government's way of preventing the publication of anything critical of the status quo. The result of this censorship was that very little literature of any value was published before 1980. Writers who wanted to express their opposition were more inclined to do so through music and song, especially protest songs. The 1970s were a productive period for songs about rebellion and revolution. African nationalist armies sang such songs as they moved around the country.

In the years after independence, many Zimbabwean writers returned from their countries of exile, while others came out of the nationalist camps in the bush. They took up the challenge of writing a new era of Zimbabwean literature in their own languages. Since 1980 Zimbabwean writers have published a large body of works in the Shona and Ndebele languages. Many have also published fiction and verse in English.

Shelves of books in a library.

CHARLES MUNGOSHI writes in English and Shona. His stories explore themes that are common to many developing countries. In one of his stories, a young man fresh out of teacher's college and starting his career cannot see what place traditional religion could have in the modern world. Although he scorns superstition and witchcraft, he finds himself asking his grandmother for a spell that will protect him when he leaves his village to work in the city.

Such a spiritual conflict is part of the larger tensions that exist between old and new, traditional and modern. Although it is a blessing to have the opportunity to go through school, in many ways it is also a curse. Education breaks down traditional ways of life and strains family relationships in several ways. As the young acquire an education, they grow up with a contrasting worldview from that of their elders.

Also, with skills that equip them for urban jobs, they become mobile and leave the countryside to live in the city, away from family. A typical character in Mungoshi's stories is torn between leaving the family in the village and forging a new identity in the city without the comfort of ancestral spirits. Mungoshi's short story collection, *The Setting Sun and the Rolling World*, examines the clash between generations, the erosion of traditional values, and the moral corruption of city life.

CHENJERAI HOVE was born in 1956. He writes novels and poems in Shona and English. Hove believes that artists have the ability and responsibility to

Two established Zimbabwean women writers are Barbara Makhalisa and Tsitsi Dangarembga. An organization for women writers was formed in 1990 to promote literature by Zimbabwean women and literacy among Zimbabwean women.

shape their country's hopes and dreams. His English novels, including the award-winning *Bones* (1988), are distinctly Zimbabwean in the traditional Shona sayings and popular myths they contain. Like the works of Charles Mungoshi, Hove's novels explore the threat of urbanization to the rural way of life.

DAMBUDZO MARECHERA was born in 1952. He gained recognition as a talented writer while teaching abroad. When he returned to Zimbabwe, he scoffed at the idea of writing for any political agenda. He felt that he should keep out of politics in order to preserve his artistic integrity. Marechera died in 1987.

One of Marechera's autobiographical works depicts a poet who is rejected by publishers because he will not write nationalistic poems in celebration of the new country. Critics attacked Marechera for not building the African spirit, and they refused to acknowledge him as an African writer. To Marechera, however, his national identity was not as relevant to his sense of self as was his identity as a writer.

DORIS LESSING was born in Persia (now Iran) on Oct 22, 1919 and raised in southern Rhodesia (now Zimbabwe). She did not have a traditional education but weaned herself on the books of many great writers and became an internationally acclaimed novelist herself. In 1950, newly returned to Britain, Lessing published her first novel, *The Grass Is Singing*, about a European woman in Africa in the context of conflicting relationships between Africans and Europeans there. Many of Lessing's works are set in the world of the European settlers in Africa and explore their relationships with the indigenous peoples.

BRUCE MOORE-KING gave a different perspective of Zimbabwe's struggle for independence in *White Man Black War*, first published in Harare in 1988. As a soldier on the European side in 1970s Zimbabwe, Moore-King experienced first-hand the horrors of war. He described in his book his anger at the violence of which he had been a part:

"I can understand, now, why our countrymen took up arms against us. If these actions and attitudes and forms of selective ignorance displayed by my tribe once caused blood and fire to spread across the land called Rhodesia … Must my tribe reinforce their Creed of racial superiority by denying these, the victors of the war, the basic humaneness of the ability to Anger?"

SHIMMER CHINODYA was born in Zimbabwe in 1957. He has written children's stories, short stories, and novels, including the prize-winning *Harvest of Thorns* (1989) which tells the coming-of-age story of a young man during the unstable period of transition from colonial Rhodesia to independent Zimbabwe. Chinodya addresses such issues as politics and religion in his stories and weaves Shona words into English prose to expose readers to Zimbabwean culture.

ALEXANDER MCCALL SMITH was born in 1948 in Bulawayo. He is most well-known for writing *The No.1 Ladies' Detective Agency* series. He is a prolific writer and has created novels, short stories, academic works as well as children's books.

INTERNET LINKS

www.nationalgallerybyo.com/

Official website of the National gallery of Bulawayo displaying various Zimbabwean artists, painters and sculptors.

www.tengenengesculpture.com/

Website of The Tengenenge Sculpture Community providing information on major exhibitions in Zimbabwe and abroad.

www.writers.co.zw/

Website for writers and poets in Zimbabwe containing useful articles, opportunities for online publishing, information on writing competitions, and more.

LEISURE

Adrenaline junkies and daring adventurists grab the chance to go white-water rafting on the Zambezi river.

11

T

THE RHODESIAN GOVERNMENT had a strong interest in sports and invested a substantial amount of money in the construction of sports facilities across the country. However, nearly all sports facilities were reserved strictly for use by the European minority.

Today sports provide the major source of leisure activity for many Zimbabweans, participant and spectator alike. The government also continues to support the country's athletes in regional and international games. Quieter forms of leisure include watching television at home or having a few drinks in a beer hall.

A multiracial circle of friends have beers while relaxing and enjoying a day out in the open waters.

TEAM SPORTS

Soccer is undoubtedly the most popular team sport in Zimbabwe. Every urban area has its own team competing in a national league. Monomotapa United, Black Mambas, CAPS United, Dynamos, and Highlanders are some of the top clubs. The national soccer team is known as The Warriors.

The soccer season runs from February to November, and the league games may attract as many as 40,000 spectators. Zimbabwe has eight main stadiums and a very big match in the Zimbabwe Premier Soccer League will attract 60,000. Rural areas have their own teams competing outside the league structure. Famous Zimbabwean soccer players include Benjani Mwaruwari, Peter Ndlovu, and Bruce Grobbelaar.

Other popular team sports are field hockey and cricket, and the national cricket squad has played well against other international teams. Rugby is also played in schools and at international competitions.

Yara Hanssen, an athlete representing Zimbabwe, participated in the equestrian jumping event during the Singapore Youth Olympic Games in 2010.

OTHER SPORTS

Golf and lawn bowling are played across the country, and horse racing is a popular spectator sport. One of the top horse-racing meets, Ascot, is named after a famous track in England.

CONSUMING THE MASS MEDIA

Zimbabweans use the mass media for entertainment as well as for information. There are around 370,000 television sets in the country and more than 1.4 million Internet users. Approximately 1.2 million visit the cinema annually. Radio is the most widespread medium, with more than a million sets distributed in both urban and rural areas.

Zimbabweans may watch television with family at home or with friends in a bar. In more rural areas, access to television can be difficult. Viewers watch many programs from the United States and Britain as well as locally produced ones. The Zimbabwe Broadcasting Corporation (ZBC) runs two television channels.

Radio listeners have many channels to choose from, such as AfroZimRadio, Zimbabwe Radio, Spot Radio, Nehanda Radio, National FM ZBC, Shaya Radio, and more. At certain times of the day, Zimbabweans can also receive broadcasts from the British Broadcasting Corporation's World Service and the Voice of America.

Reading is very much a part of leisure activity in Zimbabwe's urban areas. The local book industry is publishing a growing number of nonfiction and fiction titles, as well as poetry and drama, in Shona, Ndebele, and English. Some of the major English-language newspapers run online as well as print editions. Dailies include *The Herald* and *The Chronicle*, while weeklies include *The Sunday News*, *The Zimbabwe Independent*, and the *Sunday Mail*.

A young girl at a shop reads the newspaper to be updated on the latest happenings while awaiting customers.

GAMES

Rural Zimbabweans can have very limited access to shops that sell toys and games. Stores in the cities are far away, and the manufactured toys and games sold there are expensive.

People in the countryside thus invent their own games and toys to entertain themselves. Children may fashion from wire a small model of a car or an airplane, sometimes with movable wheels and a long metal handle that they use to steer the model as they walk.

In the game of *kudoda* (koo-DOH-dah), or *nhodo* (n-HOH-doh), a group of children sit around a scooped-out hollow in the ground about 4 inches

(10 cm) in diameter. Players take turns throwing a stone up into the air, picking up smaller stones in the hole, and catching the thrown stone before it falls into the hole. Children in other parts of the world play a similar game called jacks or five stones.

Mahumbwe (mah-HOHM-bay) is a game in which children pretend to take on adult roles, somewhat like playing house. *Mahumbwe* was originally a preparation for one's coming-of-age ceremony. When a new home was set up, a boy and a girl would take charge of it for as long as a month. The boy would go hunting, and the girl would cook. At the end of the period, there would be a special ceremony to mark their coming of age, during which participants of the ceremony would drink beer brewed by the girl.

Ndoma (ne-DOH-mah) is similar to hockey. Both boys and girls can play. Players form two teams and compete to hit a wooden ball over a boundary line.

Adults may play a game called *tsoro* (te-SOH-ROH). Essential to *tsoro* are little stones called *matombo* (mah-TOM-boh) and a wooden board with four rows of 13 or more carved holes. Each player has two rows on the board and a set of stones. Leaving the last hole in each of the rows empty, the player puts one stone in the second-to-last hole and two in each of the other holes.

The players take turns moving their stones in a counterclockwise direction and taking the opponent's stones that are already in the holes. Other versions of tsoro have different numbers of stones and rows, or use the ground instead of a wooden board.

Archeologists have discovered ancient game boards at the Khami ruins in Zimbabwe. They believe early peoples, especially royalty, used these boards as divination tools. Other such boards have been excavated from ancient sites in other parts of Africa. The ancient board games live on in the games that people living in those regions now play.

Tsoro, an ancient stone game at the Khami UNESCO World Heritage Site near Bulawayom, Zimbabwe.

INTERNET LINKS

www.zifa.org.zw/

Official website of the Zimbabwe national football team, nicknamed The Warriors, providing information about the teams including a calendar and a fan zone.

www.onlinenewspapers.com/zimbabwe.htm

Website providing links to a list of online Zimbabwean newspapers for information on local issues, politics, events, and more.

www.zbc.co.zw/

Official website of Zimbabwe Broadcasting Corporation providing the latest news on events in Zimbabwe.

FESTIVALS

A Makishi dancer dons a detailed costume and mask for a performance at a village near Victoria Falls.

12

N A COUNTRY where the many people still live and work in the countryside, the most important festivals are associated with the land. The coming of the rainy season is crucial for the growing of crops, and rainmaking ceremonies are the most significant events in the rural calendar.

Even the preparation of the seeds before the rains come can become a ceremony of its own involving the assistance of a medium.

Dancers from Zimbabwe performing at an event.

The National Arts Council of Zimbabwe has the task of promoting the arts through festivals such as the Jikinya Children's Traditional Dance Festival.

January 1	New Year's Day
March/April	Good Friday
	Holy Saturday
	Easter Sunday
	Easter Monday
April 18	Independence Day
May 1	Worker's Day
May 25	Africa Day
2nd week of August	Heroes' & Armed Forces Day
August 12	Armed Forces' Day
December 22	Unity Day
December 25	Christmas Day
December 26	Boxing Day

MAKING THE SEEDS GROW

Before the rains, the village elders and their wives pay a visit to the resident medium in a special ceremony. The proceedings begin with the medium sharing a specially prepared beer with the male visitors, who sit around the medium in a circle. They eat the evening meal in the light of a small bonfire, after which drum music begins. The women sing a traditional song that is addressed to an ancestral spirit, while others join in the ceremony by dancing and swaying to the rhythm of the drums.

Early the next morning, the villagers congregate, singing and clapping, around the entrance to the medium's home. Dressed in white, the *mhondoro* makes his dramatic appearance from the entrance. There is more singing, followed by a meeting in which various matters of local importance are discussed.

The medium delivers judgment on all matters discussed. He later collects the seeds from the households in the village, sprinkles the seeds with root plants to protect them from pests, and distributes the seeds to the villagers for planting.

RAINMAKING

Like the seed planting ceremony, the rainmaking ceremony is held to ensure a successful harvest, which the villagers depend on for their sustenance. The rainmaking ceremony takes place several days or weeks after the village elders' meeting with the medium.

The season of rainmaking festivals begins around September, when winter comes to an end and spring begins. The summer crops will not flourish without the anticipated rains, and rainmaking festivals may continue to the beginning of the following year. The year 1992 was exceptional, with the drought of the previous year continuing through the first three months of the new year. Rainmaking ceremonies were extended for a longer period than usual that year. Zimbabwe has continued to experience severe periods of drought throughout the 2000s with 2012 being a particularly dry year.

A rainmaking festival is usually prompted by the first sign of the approaching spring rains. Brewing begins, and when the beer is ready, everyone congregates at a location that is recognized for its religious significance. This may be the peak of a hill, the entrance to a cave, or a special tree. Rainmaking is a religious event for the people, who believe that their ancestral spirits influence the annual rains, which in turn affect their welfare. If the rains are late or little, the villagers see it as a sign that the ancestral spirits are unhappy or anxious about something.

The rainmaking festival is associated with darkness. It usually takes place at night and is highlighted by intense singing and dancing. The person who performs the rainmaking ceremony may be the village medium or a more senior medium for which money would have been collected at the meeting before the rainmaking ceremony. The rainmaker wears black and is believed to have the power to make rain appear by hanging out black cloths.

A nyau dancer entertains the audience at a festival.

RELIGIOUS FESTIVALS

The influence of Christianity in Zimbabwe has made Easter and Christmas important parts of the calendar of religious festivals. Even in remote, rural parts of the country, the presence of missions ensures the celebration of special church services to mark the birth, death, and resurrection of Jesus Christ. A dramatic sight in the countryside is the communal prayer gathering of thousands of white-clothed members of the Apostolic Church in a large open area to pray.

SECULAR FESTIVALS

Zimbabwe celebrates a number of secular festivals that are related to its African identity and nationhood. The country's most important civic festival takes place on April 18—Independence Day.

Members of a musical group take part in the opening number of the Harare International Festival of the Arts, involving instrument playing and singing.

Zimbabwe's first Independence Day was attended by an array of international figures, including the prime minister of Jamaica and the famous Jamaican musician, Bob Marley. Marley and his band had previously released records that supported the African nationalists who fought the European government in Zimbabwe.

THE HARARE INTERNATIONAL FESTIVAL OF THE ARTS

The Harare International Festival of the Arts is one of the most important and diverse cultural events organized in Africa. In 2012, it was in its 13th year and has come to be seen as a positive symbol for Zimbabwe and its people against the backdrop of its social and political problems. This annual event is held over 6 days usually in April/May and brings together the very best of Zimbabwean, regional, and international arts and culture through an exciting and broad program which includes theatre, dance, music, circus, street performance, spoken word, craft, and visual arts.

INTERNET LINKS

www.hifa.co.zw/

Website of the Harare International Festival of the Arts, a yearly culture and music celebration offering a historic background, news and articles, and a program schedule.

www.zimfest.org/

Website of the largest annual gathering in North America of students, teachers, performers, and fans of Zimbabwean music.

http://kadmusarts.com/countries/Zimbabwe.html

Website providing a comprehensive listing of all the current festivals happening in Zimbabwe throughout the year.

FOOD

Bunches of oranges for sale at a fruit and vegetable market.

I N ZIMBABWE, FOOD serves a strictly functional purpose. Unlike French or Japanese cuisine, for example, Zimbabwean cooking does not show much concern for the aesthetics of presentation. Nor are there a similar variety of ingredients or flavors.

Nearly a century of colonization has added little to the character of Zimbabwean food. However, the quality of meat in the country is very high, and a Zimbabwean steak is one of the country's tastiest dishes.

Supermarkets in the capital sell canned, bottled, dried, frozen, and other processed and packaged foods that are found in supermarkets in modern cities around the world. However, the traditional Zimbabwean diet is based on corn, vegetables, and some meat.

Simple food items stocked on shelves at a supermarket in Bulawayo.

A typical Zimbabwean meal consists of *sadza*—porridge made from maize or cornmeal—which is eaten at least twice a day with other savoury dishes such as meat, fish, and vegetables.

13

CORN

Corn is an important staple in Zimbabwe, being nutritious and readily available. It consists largely of starch, which provides a valuable supply of glucose, but corn is also a source of protein and oil, providing many of the body's essential dietary needs.

Corn is at the heart of traditional Zimbabwean cooking and is used as a core ingredient in many Zimbabwean dishes. Corn is used to make *sadza*, a thick corn porridge that is an essential part of the daily diet. Freshly cooked *sadza* is sold in trains and bus stations, and every rural Zimbabwean knows how to make good *sadza*—by cooking slowly to bring out the taste. Corn is also used to make a thick, white, and rather chewy beer. It is a potent drink that retains the protein of corn.

Corn is so important to Zimbabwe that during the food crisis of 2002, the government rejected genetically engineered corn from the United States for fear that the corn would contaminate domestic yields.

A woman transfers a bountiful harvest of corn from the transported sack to a bowl to be cooked.

MEALS AND SNACKS

Apart from *sadza*, a meal usually includes a meat-and-vegetable stew. While the meat is often plain in taste and appearance, the range of vegetables contributes a lot to the taste and color of the meal. Pumpkin, corn-on-the-cob, and butternut squash are common.

People living in the cities have more international food choices. Restaurants offer foreign cuisines, and fast-food outlets serve burgers and french fries.

A rich variety of fruit is readily available. Market stalls are filled with guavas, mangoes, ladyfinger, bananas, papayas, and other kinds of wild fruit that may be less familiar to foreigners. One of the most popular foods is *mazhanje* or wild loquats which usually are eaten fresh after a meal.

The staple diet of the Ndebele people is based on cereals that are cooked to make a thick porridge known as isitshwala *(is-eet-KWA-lah).* Isitshwala *is eaten with milk and vegetables (right).*

The Ndebele have a long tradition of hunting, going back to the early days before they settled as farmers. They used dogs to trace the scent of their quarry and knobkerrie *(KNOB-ker-ree) clubs to deliver the killing blow. According to tradition, the best meat from a hunting expedition was claimed by the hunter whose* knobkerrie *or spear killed the animal.*

Eating cured meat is another tradition in Ndebele culture, although it is no longer as common as it once was. The meat is flavored with salt and herbs, and sometimes left to dry in the sun before being eaten.

Zimbabwean snacks are often deep-fried, but there are also baked varieties, such as sweet potato cookies.

BARBECUES AND BREAD

Barbecues, or *braaivleis* (brah-IV-lees), are common in Zimbabwe. The cooked steak is often eaten with *boerewors* (BOH-vorz), or spicy sausage, and a bowl of *sadza*. *Sosaties* (soh-SAH-teez) are pieces of mutton that have been seasoned overnight with curry sauce and tamarind, and then barbecued or fried.

Rural Zimbabweans may barbecue inside the home, which is often a simple structure of upright poles plastered with clay and topped with a conical roof of thatched grass. The kitchen section may consist of three stones around a fire to support the cooking pots. With no windows or chimney, the smoke from the fire is left to find its way out through gaps between the roof and the upper edge of the walls.

Bread was traditionally baked thick and almost black, with all the natural fiber retained. Today, most Zimbabweans eat white bread.

FOOD CRISES

A makeshift grill made of wood and wire mesh where food is cooked and served to villagers.

In a country that is so dependent on agriculture, prolonged drought has devastating consequences. With drastically reduced crop yields, people cannot feed themselves or their animals, and even staple foods such as corn have to be imported.

Millions of Zimbabwean men, women, and children have suffered from hunger and malnutrition during the country's recent food crises. Monthly corn handouts from the government and relief organizations were not able to cope with the dietary demands of the large families in affected villages. Even wild fruit and water were in short supply in certain areas. The country went from being a grain exporter to importing staple foods, which still fell far short of consumption needs. The last drought that led to such a severe crisis occurred two decades earlier, in 1992. In 2012, Zimbabwe again faced a desperate food shortage as 30 percent of the maize crop was damaged because of drought. Zimbabwe remains plagued by droughts at present.

The droughts triggered a web of related problems. Crop shortages resulted in seed shortages. Shortages of seeds and fertilizers resulted in less planting

Beer halls are large covered areas dedicated to the consumption of beer. They have a loud and very masculine atmosphere.

Nevertheless, beer halls function as important centers of social life for working-class Zimbabweans. Besides branded beers, the halls also serve chibuku *(chi-BOO-koo).* Chibuku *is known as "The Beer of Africa," a beer that is brewed from corn and served in large containers.*

and poorer harvests. Poor harvests, exacerbated by a lack of rainfall, resulted in a shortage of food crops, which in turn led to skyrocketing prices that have made basic foodstuffs very expensive. Bread prices, for example, soared as Zimbabweans turned to bread as an alternative to cornmeal.

In addition to natural causes, human factors also contributed to reduced crop yields and further complicated the country's food crisis. Violent takeovers of commercial farms were one of the major causes of the country's reduced agricultural productivity.

DRINKS

Beer is the most common alcoholic drink in Zimbabwe. Canned beers display many of the brand names that are familiar to people from North America and Europe. Beer is served almost everywhere in Zimbabwe, including beer halls and shebeens. A shebeen is an illegal drinking party, and small shebeens are common in the more densely populated urban centers.

The brewing and drinking of beer has an important ceremonial role and social significance. For example, beer is often an essential prerequisite in

A hungry child is given a half-eaten cob of corn. Scarcity of food is an issue for many local folks.

Zimbabweans wait in a long line to purchase food.

animist rituals. Beer is also brewed and drunk to mark special occasions, such as the birth of a child.

Zimbabwean nonalcoholic drinks include *mazoe* (mah-ZOH-ee), which is a lime or orange squash made from fruit with no sugar or chemicals added. There is also the Malawi shandy, a mixture of ginger beer, soda water, and lemon, served cold.

TO EAT OR NOT TO EAT?

Zimbabweans traditionally do not eat rats, bats, hyenas, leopards, lions, crocodiles, and other predatory or nocturnal animals. Generally, food taboos in the country are based on the clan system of the Shona and Ndebele. There is a strict rule that people belonging to a particular clan must never eat the animal after which their clan is named. That animal's flesh becomes a forbidden food, and it is believed that if a clan member eats it, strange punishments will befall him or her. For example, the person's teeth may fall out, or a sudden sickness may afflict him or her.

The taboo on the clan animal is central to the whole notion of clan identity. When asked how they know what clan they belong to, Zimbabweans may explain that they once ate some mutton and immediately fell ill. That, they would explain, showed that they were members of the sheep clan.

Different clans have differing rules on their relationship with the clan animal. If a person is a member of the pig clan, he or she can never ever eat pork. A person who belongs to the elephant clan avoids the animal.

A possible explanation for such food taboos is that the custom has developed over centuries in order to prevent a shortage of any particular species of animal. If each clan avoids hunting a certain animal, then the practice ensures an equal killing rate across a range of species.

On the other hand, the traditional Zimbabwean diet includes some rather exotic items. A species of caterpillar is cooked in ash to make a snack, and the dried version—called *madora*—is sold in stores. Readily available and affordable, it is a good source of protein for poorer Zimbabweans.

Game meats are common. Outside of clan restrictions, Zimbabweans eat antelope and giraffe meat and birds such as pheasant and quail. Rodents other than rats may be smoked, roasted, or boiled.

INTERNET LINKS

www.foodbycountry.com/Spain-to-Zimbabwe-Cumulative-Index/Zimbabwe.html

Website providing information about Zimbabwe's food history, celebration food, politics and nutrition and more.

www.numbeo.com/food-prices/country_result.jsp?country=Zimbabwe

Website providing information about food prices in Zimbabwe including money needed to buy basic food items.

www.celtnet.org.uk/recipes/zimbabwe.php

Website of Celtnet Recipes section with a variety of interesting recipes from Zimbabwe.

CHICKEN AND VEGETABLE SOUP

A favourite amongst Zimbabweans, this hearty and delicious soup serves 6.

1 tablespoon (15 ml) olive oil

1 medium onion, diced

4 cups (1 L) vegetable stock, divided

½ cup (125 ml) peanut butter

2 cups (500 ml) canned diced tomatoes, with juices

Pinch of crushed red pepper flakes, or more to taste

1 cup (250 ml) finely chopped cabbage

1 cup (250 ml) chopped sweet potato

1 cup (250 ml) peeled and chopped carrot

1 cup (250 ml) peeled and chopped turnip

1 cup (250 ml) chopped okra

1 cup (250 ml) chopped cooked chicken, or to taste

Heat the olive oil over medium heat in a large soup pot; cook and stir the onion in the hot oil until translucent, about 5 minutes. Whisk ½ cup of vegetable stock and the peanut butter into the onions until the mixture is smooth. Beat in remaining vegetable stock, diced tomatoes with their liquid, and crushed red pepper flakes; bring to a boil, reduce heat to medium low, and cook at a simmer for 30 minutes, stirring occasionally. Stir in the cabbage, sweet potato, carrot, and turnip; simmer, stirring occasionally, until the vegetables are tender, about 30 more minutes. Stir in the okra and chicken and simmer until the okra is tender, about 30 additional minutes.

PEANUT BUTTER VEGETABLE STEW

Often eaten with sadza *or cornmeal porridge, peanuts are a very common ingredient in Zimbabwean cooking. Serves 4.*

1 bunch of silver beet or a vegetable leaf that is a little tougher like kale

3 tablespoons (45 ml) of peanut putter

1 cup (250 ml) water

1 large tomato, cored, chopped

1 medium onion chopped

3 tablespoons (45 ml) smooth peanut butter

pinch of salt

Shred 1 bunch of silver beet, kale, or an alternative, removing the tough stems. Steam in ¼ cup of salted water, reserving a little water. Add tomatoes and onion. Stir and allow simmering. Add peanut butter stirring frequently until greens have a creamy consistency.

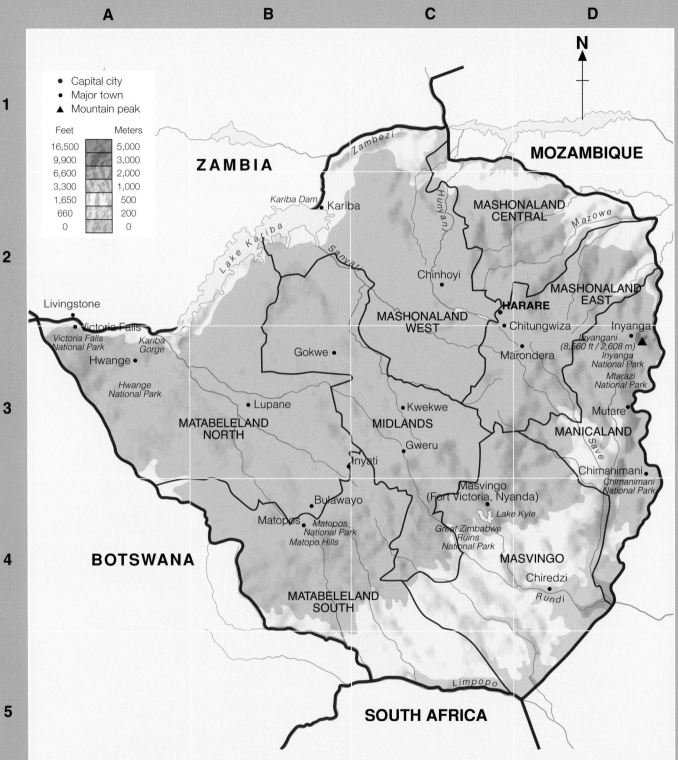

MAP OF ZIMBABWE

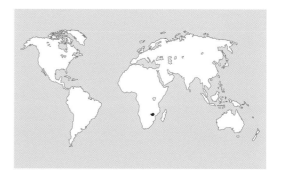

ECONOMIC ZIMBABWE

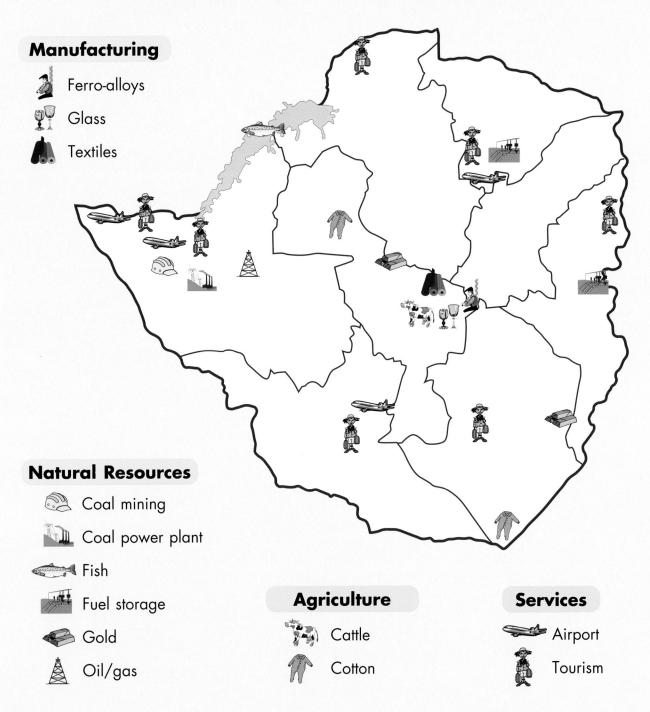

Manufacturing
- Ferro-alloys
- Glass
- Textiles

Natural Resources
- Coal mining
- Coal power plant
- Fish
- Fuel storage
- Gold
- Oil/gas

Agriculture
- Cattle
- Cotton

Services
- Airport
- Tourism

ABOUT THE ECONOMY

OVERVIEW

Zimbabwe has paid a high economic price for its participation in the war in the Democratic Republic of the Congo from 1998 to 2002. The economy suffered further as a result of its government's land reform program, which essentially destroyed its valuable commercial farming industry. Zimbabwe experienced a severe economic contraction between 1998 to 2008, coupled with hyperinflation. Zimbabwe's economy recorded real growth of more than 9 percent per year in 2011 before slowing to 5 percent in 2012, due to a poor harvest and low diamond revenues. If the country is to maintain and promote further growth, it has to overcome several significant obstacles such as improving its infrastructure, implementing clearer economic regulation and policies, managing its massive public external debt and high unemployment, and working with the pressure of indigenization.

CURRENCY

1 Zimbabwean dollar (ZWD) = 100 cents
1 USD = 361.90 ZWD (October 2013)
Note: The USD was adopted as a legal currency in 2009, as the Zimbabwean dollar is virtually worthless due to hyperinflation.
Notes: 1, 2, 5, 10, 20, 50, 100 dollars
Coins: 1, 5, 10, 20, 50 cents; 1 dollar

GROSS DOMESTIC PRODUCT (GDP)

$7.366 billion
Per capita: $600 (2012 estimate)
Note: this is an inaccurate estimate as the Zimbabwean dollar was taken out of circulation in 2009.

GDP GROWTH RATE

4.4 percent (2012 estimate)

GDP SECTORS

Agriculture 20.3 percent, industry 25.1 percent, services 54.6 percent (2012 estimate)

WORK FORCE

3.931 million (2012 estimate)

UNEMPLOYMENT RATE

80 percent (2012 estimate)

INFLATION RATE

8.2 percent (2012 estimate)

POPULATION BELOW POVERTY LINE

81 percent (2012 estimate)

EXTERNAL DEBT

$8.767 billion (2012 estimate)

AGRICULTURAL PRODUCTS

Coffee, corn, cotton, peanuts, sugarcane, tobacco, wheat; goats, pigs, sheep

INDUSTRIES

Beverage, cement, clothing and footwear, chemicals, fertilizer, foodstuffs, mining (coal, gold, platinum, copper, nickel, tin, diamonds, clay, numerous metallic and non-metallic ores), steel, wood products

CULTURAL ZIMBABWE

Mana Pools
Visitors can go on a walking safari to see a wide range of wild animals such as the rare black rhinoceros, or ride canoes in the Zambezi and get close to menacing hippos.

National Museums
Harare is Zimbabwe's city of museums. Visitors learn about natural history at the Queen Victoria Museum, and see art exhibits at the National Gallery. The National Botanical Gardens has a wide range of indigenous flora.

Lake Kariba
Visitors enjoy fishing safaris from houseboats on Lake Kariba. Home to a vibrant array of fish such as catfish and bream, Lake Kariba attracts fishing enthusiasts to an annual tiger fish tournament.

Victoria Falls
More than 150 million years old, Victoria Falls is one of the world's largest waterfalls, falling from a height exceeding 300 feet (90 km).

Hwange
Zimbabwe's oldest, largest, and most famous national park is home to about 20,000 elephants and many other wild animals, such as antelopes, buffalos, crocodiles, lions, and rhinos.

Matopo Hills
Billions of years old, the hills of granite and gneiss near Bulawayo are known for their interesting rock formations, such as ball-like boulders balancing one on top of another.

Great Zimbabwe
With high curved walls erected without mortar, the ruins of the medieval city of Great Zimbabwe, after which independent Zimbabwe was named, are the second most popular tourist destination in the country.

Mount Inyangani
Adventurers may climb Zimbabwe's highest mountain, rising to 8,560 feet (2,608 m), not only for the physical challenge but also to test tales about climbers who went missing on Inyangani.

ABOUT THE CULTURE

OFFICIAL NAME
Republic of Zimbabwe

NATIONAL FLAG
Seven equal horizontal bands of green, yellow, red, black, red, yellow, and green with a white isosceles triangle edged in black with its base on the hoist side; a yellow Zimbabwe bird representing the long history of the country is superimposed on a red five-pointed star in the center of the triangle, which symbolizes peace; green represents agriculture, yellow mineral wealth, red the blood shed to achieve independence, and black stands for the native people

CAPITAL
Harare

MAJOR CITIES
Bulawayo, Harare

ADMINISTRATIVE DIVISIONS
Bulawayo, Harare, Manicaland, Mashonaland Central, Mashonaland East, Mashonaland West, Masvingo, Matabeleland North, Matabeleland South, Midlands

POPULATION
12,619,600 (2012 estimate)

POPULATION GROWTH RATE
2.27 percent (2013 estimate)

LIFE EXPECTANCY
51.82 years (2012 estimate)

BIRTH RATE
32.41 births/1,000 population (2013 estimate)

DEATH RATE
11.4 deaths/1,000 population (2013 estimate)

INFANT MORTALITY RATE
27.25 deaths/1,000 live births (2013 estimate)

ETHNIC GROUPS
Shona 82 percent, Ndebele 14 percent, other African 2 percent; mixed and Asian 1 percent, European and other white less than 1 percent

MAJOR LANGUAGES
English (official), Shona, Sindebele or Ndebele; minor dialects

LITERACY RATE
83.6 percent of adults more than 15 years old can read and write (2011 estimate)

RELIGIONS
Syncretic (part Christian, part indigenous beliefs) 50 percent, Christian 25 percent, indigenous beliefs 24 percent, Muslim and other 1 percent

TIMELINE

IN ZIMBABWE	IN THE WORLD

8000 B.C.
San hunter-gatherers populate the area.

A.D. 300
Bantu peoples arrive.

A.D. 500
Shona peoples grow sorghum and millet, and raise cattle.

1150–1450
The stone city of Great Zimbabwe is built.

1206–1368
Genghis Khan unifies the Mongols and starts conquest of the world.

1512
The Portuguese arrive, marking the start of European interest in the area.

1789–99
The French Revolution

1840
Mzilikazi, a former warrior in Shaka Zulu's army, establishes a Ndebele community.

1870
Lobengula becomes king of the Ndebele.

1890
Cecil Rhodes establishes Fort Victoria.

1895
The Ndebele are defeated.

1896
The First Chimurenga

1914
World War I begins.

1923
Rhodesia becomes Southern Rhodesia.

1939
World War II begins.

1957
The African National Congress (ANC) is formed.

1961
The Zimbabwe African National Union (ZANU) is formed.

1965
Prime Minister Ian Douglas Smith signs a Unilateral Declaration of Independence.

1972
The Second Chimurenga

1980
Robert Mugabe is elected prime minister of independent Zimbabwe.

1987
Mugabe becomes president.

1989
ZANU and ZAPU merge to form the Zimbabwe African National Union Patriotic Front (ZANU-PF).

1992
Severe drought leads to a food crisis.

IN ZIMBABWE	IN THE WORLD
1998 Violent seizure of European farms begins.	
1999 The Movement for Democratic Change (MDC) opposition party is formed.	
2002 Food crisis; Mugabe wins presidential elections amid accusations of vote rigging. European Union (EU) imposes sanctions.	
2003 Opposition Movement for Democratic Change (MDC) leader Morgan Tsvangirai arrested twice over an alleged plot to kill President Mugabe. Zimbabwe pulls out of Commonwealth.	**2003** War in Iraq begins.
2004 Opposition leader Morgan Tsvangirai acquitted of treason charges.	**2004** Eleven Asian countries are hit by giant tsunami, killing at least 225,000 people.
2005 Urban "clean-up" of tens of thousands of shanty dwellings and illegal street stalls leaves an estimated 700,000 people homeless. Ruling Zanu-PF party wins an overwhelming majority.	**2005** Hurricane Katrina devastates the Gulf Coast of the United States.
2006 Year-on-year inflation exceeds 1,000 percent. Riots against the government's handling of the economic crisis. Ruling ZANU-PF extends Mugabe's rule by two years.	
2007 Rallies and demonstrations banned for three months. Warnings of power cuts for up to 20 hours a day while electricity is diverted toward agriculture.	
2008 Presidential and parliamentary elections. Robert Mugabe retained presidency and Morgan Tsvangirai made prime minister.	**2008** Earthquake in Sichuan, China, kills 67,000 people.
2009 Government allows use of foreign currencies to try to stem hyperinflation. Tsvangirai is sworn in as prime minister.	**2009** Outbreak of flu virus H1N1 around the world
2010 Ruling Zanu-PF party nominates President Mugabe as candidate for next presidential race.	**2011** Twin earthquake and tsunami disasters strike northeast Japan, leaving more than 14,000 dead and thousands more missing.
2013 Robert Mugabe claims a seventh term as president after an electoral victory.	

GLOSSARY

Bantu (BAHN-too)
An ethnic or linguistic group in Africa. Examples of Bantu peoples or languages include Ndebele and Shona.

chimurenga (chim-oo-RENG-ah)
War of liberation.

Communal lands
Reserves where farming families live and grow crops for their own use, selling off excess crops at the local market.

hosho (HOH-shoh)
A musical instrument consisting of a gourd that is partially filled with dried seeds. When the gourd is shaken, the seeds produce a rattling sound.

kudoda (koo-DOH-dah)
A game in which players take turns to grab stones from a hole in the ground while throwing and hopping another stone.

marimba
A xylophone with wooden strips, each producing a different tone when struck with a rubber mallet.

mazoe (mah-ZOH-ee)
A nonalcoholic drink made from lime or orange with no sugar or chemicals added.

mbira (merh-BIRAH)
A thumb piano with a wooden soundboard and metal strips of varying lengths that are plucked to produce a melody.

mhondoro (meh-HOHN-doh-roh)
The spirit of a dead tribal chief.

Mzilikazi (m-zee-lee-KAH-zee)
King of the Ndebele; lived from 1790 to 1868.

Ndebele (en-deh-BEE-lee)
The second largest ethnic group in Zimbabwe, related to the Zulus of South Africa.

ndoma (ne-DOH-mah)
A game similar to hockey in which two teams hit a wooden ball over a dividing line.

sadza (SAHD-zah)
A porridge made from corn that forms the staple diet of most Zimbabweans.

San (SAHN)
A people that lived in Africa for thousands of years before the Portuguese arrived in the 15th century.

sarungano (sahr-oon-GAH-noh)
A storyteller, traditionally an elder.

Shona (SHOH-nah)
The largest ethnic group in Zimbabwe.

tsoro (te-SOH-ROH)
A wooden board game in which players move stones from one hole to another, collecting their opponents' stones i n the process.

Vapostori
Members of the Apostolic Church in Zimbabwe.

FOR FURTHER INFORMATION

BOOKS

Baughan, Michael Gray. *Zimbabwe: Africa,Continent in the Balalnce.* Bromall: Mason Crest Publishers, 2005.

Barclay, Philip. *Zimbabwe: Years of Hope and Despair.* London: Bloomsbury Publishing, 2011.

Blair, David. *Degrees in Violence: Robert Mugabe and the Struggle for Power in Zimbabwe.* Continuum Publishing Group, 2003.

Lessing, Dorris. *The Grass is Singing: A Novel.* Perennial Press, 2000.

Meredith, Martin. *Mugabe: Power, Plunder and the Struggle for Zimbabwe's Future.* New York: Public Affairs,US, 2007.

Murray,Paul. *Zimbabwe (Brandt Travel Guides).* Chalfont St.Peter: Brandt Travel Guides, 2010.

Raftopoulos,Brian and Mlambo, Alois. *Becoming Zimbabwe: A History from the Pre-Colonial Period to 2008.* Harare: Weaver Press, 2009.

Wallace, Jason. *Out of Shadows.* London: Andersen Press, 2010.

Williams, Lizzie. *Zimbabwe Handbook.* Bath: Footprint Travel Guides, 2010.

DVDS/FILMS

Zimbabwe Gem of Africa. TravelVideoStore.com, 2010.

Nature Wonders Victoria falls Zimbabwe. TravelVideoStore.com, 2005.

Mugabe and The White African. Dogwoof, 2009.

Zimbabwe Countdown. HB Films, 2010.

MUSIC

Batonga across the waters. SWP Records,2009.

Bulawayo Jazz-Hugh Tracey. SWP Records, 2009.

Document: Zimbabwe. Womad Document, 2001.

Mbira: Healing Music of Zimbabwe. Relaxation, 2000.

Tales of Zimbabwe. Sheer Sound, 2006.

Zimbabwe Shona Mbira Music. Nonesuch, 2002.

BIBLIOGRAPHY

BOOKS

Anderson, Daphne. *The Toe Rags: A Memoir.* Vermont: Trafalgar, 1990.

Barnes-Svarney, Patricia. *Zimbabwe.* NY: Chelsea House, 1989.

Baynham, Simon. *Zimbabwe in Transition.* Pennsylvania: Coronet Books, 1990.

Beach, David. *War and Politics in Zimbabwe 1840-1900.* Gweru: Mambo Press, 1986.

Cheney, Patricia. *The Land and People of Zimbabwe.* NY: Harper Collins, 1990.

Frederikse, Julie. *None But Ourselves.* NY: Viking Penguin, 1982.

Garlake, Peter. *The Hunter's Vision.* London: British Museum Press, 1995.

Kandimba,VT. *Folk Tales from Zimbabwe.* Bloomington: Xlibris, Corp., 1997.

Lan, David. *Guns & Rain: Guerillas & Spirit Mediums in Zimbabwe.* University of California Press, 1985.

Lessing, Doris. *African Laughter: Four Visits to Zimbabwe.* NY: Harper Collins, 1992.

McLaughlin, Janice. *On the Frontline: Catholic Missions in Zimbabwe's Liberation War.* Harare: Baobab Books, 1996.

Moore-King, Bruce. *White Man Black War.* Harare: Baobab Books, 1988.

Mungoshi, Charles. *Waiting for the Rain. Southern African Political Economy Series.* Harare: Zimbabwe Publishing House, 1991.

Palmer, Robin and Isobel Birch. *Zimbabwe: A Land Divided.* Oxfam Country Profiles Series. Oxford: Oxfam Publications, 1992.

Ponter, Laura J., et al. *Spirits in Stone: Zimbabwe Shona Sculpture.* Ukama Press, 1997.

Ranger, Terence. *Voices from the Rocks: Nature, Culture and History in the Matopos.* Harare: Baobob Books, 1999.

Vaughan, Richard. *Zimbabwe.* Maryland: Roman & Littlefield, Publishers Inc, 1992.

Worth, Richard. *Robert Mugabe of Zimbabwe.* NJ: Julian Messner, 1990.

WEBSITES

Central Intelligence Agency World Factbook (select Zimbabwe from the country list). www.cia.gov/library/publications/the-world-factbook/geos/zi.html

Hwange Conservation Society. www.hwangecons.org.uk

Lonely Planet World Guide: Destination Zimbabwe. www.lonelyplanet.com/zimbabwe

Parliament of Zimbabwe. www.parlzim.gov.zw

U.S. Department of State human rights report on Zimbabwe. www.state.gov/g/drl/rls/hrrpt/2001/af/8411.htm

The World Bank Group (type "Zimbabwe" in the search box). http://web.worldbank.org/

Zimbabwe Government Online. www.zim.gov.zw/

Zimbabwean Music Festival. www.zimfest.org

Zimbabwe Tourism Authority. www.zimbabwetourism.net/

INDEX

INDEX